Global White Supremacy

Global White Supremacy

Anti-Blackness and the University as Colonizer

CHRISTOPHER S. COLLINS, CHRISTOPHER B. NEWMAN, AND ALEXANDER JUN

Rutgers University Press
New Brunswick, Camden, and Newark, New Jersey
London and Oxford

Rutgers University Press is a department of Rutgers, The State University of New Jersey, one of the leading public research universities in the nation. By publishing worldwide, it furthers the university's mission of dedication to excellence in teaching, scholarship, research, and clinical care.

Library of Congress Cataloging-in-Publication Data

Names: Collins, Christopher S., author. | Newman, Christopher B., author. | Jun, Alexander, author.
Title: Global white supremacy : anti-blackness and the university as colonizer / Christopher S. Collins, Christopher B. Newman, Alexander Jun.
Description: New Brunswick, NJ : Rutgers University Press, 2023. | Includes bibliographical references and index.
Identifiers: LCCN 2022038516 | ISBN 9781978831841 (paperback) | ISBN 9781978831858 (hardback) | ISBN 9781978831865 (epub) | ISBN 9781978831889 (pdf)
Subjects: LCSH: Racism in higher education. | Racism against Black people. | Education, Higher—Social aspects. | White nationalism. | Education, Colonial.
Classification: LCC LC212.4 .C65 2023 | DDC 378.0089—dc23/eng/20220922
LC record available at https://lccn.loc.gov/2022038516

A British Cataloging-in-Publication record for this book is available from the British Library.

Copyright © 2023 by Christopher S. Collins, Christopher B. Newman, and Alexander Jun
All rights reserved

No part of this book may be reproduced or utilized in any form or by any means, electronic or mechanical, or by any information storage and retrieval system, without written permission from the publisher. Please contact Rutgers University Press, 106 Somerset Street, New Brunswick, NJ 08901. The only exception to this prohibition is "fair use" as defined by U.S. copyright law.

References to internet websites (URLs) were accurate at the time of writing. Neither the author nor Rutgers University Press is responsible for URLs that may have expired or changed since the manuscript was prepared.

rutgersuniversitypress.org

For Kristy, Mateo, and Adela—may we always be peacemakers.
Christopher Collins

To my mother, Cheryl, and father, Calvin, thank you for your many sacrifices past and present.
Christopher Newman

To Jeany, Natalia, Isaiah, and Jeremiah: Act justly, love mercy, and walk humbly with your God.
Alexander Jun

Contents

Preface: Who We Are and Why It Matters		ix
Introduction		1

Part I Ideology   17

1. Tools of Invasion: A Disposition to Inhabit the Globe   19
2. Homeland, Diaspora, and Traveling Whiteness   37
3. The University as Colonizer and Carrier of White Dominance   53

Part II Case Studies   69

4. Dominant White Minorities and Invasion in Southern Africa   73
5. Shades of Advantage in Brazil   91
6. Empty Treaties and Occupied Land in Oceania   107

Conclusion: Decolonized Past and Future   125

Acknowledgments   135
Notes   137
Index   147

Preface

Who We Are and Why It Matters

We examined our roles as researchers carefully throughout the study. The process of research across regions and cultures held a mirror up to our assumptions and reminded us of the ways in which our understanding of knowledge production has been both liberatory and oppressive depending on the way it was used. By exploring human interactions over time, we are consistently confronted with the roles of race and knowledge, which brought us to the point of exploring White supremacy as a global concept. There is no singular White perspective, just as there is not a monolithic way of knowing any ethnic group. Although the dominant paradigms in research on culture help create categories in the literature, they cannot be applied bluntly to peoples and societies. Part of our process was to continually excavate our own perspectives, enhance our cultural humility/emotional intelligence, and recognize our limitations. These reflections were done with a transnational racial optic by asking the questions: How are we viewed as researchers within different racial categories in each of the three regions? How did we receive or interpret the culture through our various lenses?

We traveled multiple times to South Africa (and to neighboring Zimbabwe and Zambia), Oceania (including Australia and Aotearoa/New Zealand), and Brazil. These three regions in the Southern Hemisphere (and politically, the Global South) have a unique connection in highlighting the ways in which European perspectives moved into regions of the world through settler colonialism and multiple tools of invasion, and then were preserved by the ultimate knowledge-producing/distributing institutions known as universities. In our own educational histories, we all went to undergraduate and graduate institutions in Southern California (UCSB, USC, and Pepperdine for undergraduate degrees and UCLA and USC for graduate). At each stage of our education, we understood the university to be an asset to society. In this study, we excavate the role of the university in a global and historical way with a racial lens. The diffusion of White supremacy from Europe was enhanced by a global anti-Blackness, which is now interwoven into the curricula, research methods, and epistemological dispositions of the Western academic canon.

Our travels and studies were purposefully focused on universities as social institutions, but in order to examine them, we had to take an in-depth look at the society and history surrounding them. We also went to great lengths to unlearn and relearn about knowledges that are both recognized and ignored by the academic canon. As a result, this book will go several sections without mentioning the university proper in an effort to understand its roots and to center the knowledges of first peoples and nations, their methods, and their histories. Race is woven throughout conceptualizations of settler colonialism and knowledge construction. We begin with our own self-examination and excavation of the concepts of race and education through our journeys and studies in the Southern Hemisphere.

Christopher S. Collins

As I move around the globe into different neighborhoods, communities, countries, and regions, my White man tourist/traveler/researcher lens continues to evolve. My first lengthy experiences outside of the United States were all in Europe while working on an undergraduate degree. As a sociology major, I became concerned with stratification, inequality, poverty, and racism, so my traveler lens evolved with a "helping" focus. I applied for the Peace Corps (a volunteer initiative of the U.S. government) and was assigned to the island nation of Vanuatu, which is 500 miles north of Aotearoa in Oceania. The few months that I spent there cemented my interest in the many things that I did not understand and twisted my understanding of the narrow, paternalistic, and technocratic helping function of the West to the rest. I did not understand the concept of settler colonialism and certainly did not understand the global reach of White supremacy. A few years later in graduate school, while studying international development organizations like the World Bank and the United States Agency for International Development and their role in higher education, I observed the function of universities and coloniality in Thailand, Uganda, and Ethiopia.

When this book project began, I spent several years making annual trips to South Africa (and Zimbabwe and Zambia). My first time landing in Cape Town and driving from the airport to the city, I observed the townships, which are miles of informal structures that are residue from the apartheid era of sequestering Black Africans into districts where they could be retrieved for

FIGURE 1 Sign from an apartheid-era township checkpoint in South Africa. (Photo by author.)

specific labor needs. They were designed with one entrance/exit with a checkpoint. Only a short distance away, the road leads to a wealth capital of the continent with majestic views of the ocean and mountains, and world-class hotels, restaurants, monuments, and universities.

Though I was jarred by the stark difference, I did not yet have the ability or capacity to think about how the people in those places would perceive me. On my first visit, I remember seeing advertisements for township tours, which I originally dismissed as poverty tourism. When preparing to take doctoral students on a study-away trip, I initially thought there was no way I would get to the townships other than through the tours I had dismissed, but a professor friend challenged me on my assumptions. After being connected with Vuyelwa Jacobs, a community activist and cultural guide, our group ended up going to church in Gugulethu and driving through Langa. We stopped to eat at a famous restaurant called Mzoli's. It is a BBQ place where you choose your raw meat and then take a seat outside and wait for it to come out with sides of pap (maize in the style of grits) and chakalaka. Our students timidly exited the van and then went inside. Our driver noted that he was going to stay to "protect" the van. I asked if I could bring him some food, and in a thick Afrikaner accent, he said, "I don't eat that dog food." It was unsettling to hear him say that in the moment, but in my multiple subsequent trips and reflections,

I continue to think about how his disgust was a representation of a White system, and how my role and presence as a White researcher were cast through that system as well.

Throughout our multiple visits, we were interacting with Black South Africans in Cape Town, most of whom were food servers, but most of the professors we met with were White. This was a little different from our experience in Aotearoa (New Zealand). While at a museum in Auckland, we saw a group of Māori who were there to perform a haka. They were wearing traditional Māori clothing and were smoking across the street. As I was strolling on a walkway to get to an entry point, someone yelled, "Get out of the street f-cking *pakeha*!" (a term for White people). A few moments later, Alex joined the group by requesting a light for his clove cigarette—it was an entry point that promoted a great conversation about race relations in Aotearoa. He told the group about our study and listened to their comments about the ways in which race was being ignored in the current political context.

The next day I was at a university trying to create a connection with a Māori center as a potential educational partner. Someone from the center agreed to meet with me, and upon finding out that there were no Indigenous students from our group, the person said, "Then you're wasting my time. Every minute I spend sitting here with someone like you wanting to do the things you do, I'm not working with our Indigenous students, who are being ignored and underserved in other areas of the university." At that moment I had two competing instincts operating like little voices on my shoulders. The first one said, "Get up and leave—you are the invader, and you can end the violence by evacuating." My second instinct was based on the idea that I was still a guest, meaning, you do not just excuse yourself; you cannot get up from the table and leave. Either action could be seen as a sign of respect or disrespect. I delayed making any kind of move and tried to stay in the space while waiting for the next cue. What happened next is that the person had arranged for me to meet with three other people in the university. It seemed contradictory until I learned more about the haka, and then it felt paradoxical.

In a *pōwhiri*, a welcoming ceremony, Māori perform the haka, which is characterized by images like the tongue out, eyes rolled back, intense chanting, spears, and gestures connoting a confrontation. The first part of the ceremony is a test to see if the visitors are coming with humility and in peace. You can react to the initial chants in fear and leave, or show humility and stay, proceeding in peace. When I chose to stay, although unsure of myself, it linked me back to other moments of deep learning throughout Oceania.

When I was in the Peace Corps in Vanuatu, I was disillusioned in many ways, but one of the ways was the recognition of the problematic assumptions of benevolence. I realized that we were not there helping but rather learning and spreading capitalism with Western knowledge assumptions. I left the assignment early due to a combination of disillusionment and a family issue that left me feeling unsettled about being so far away. A few years later, after completing a PhD at UCLA, I had my first faculty job at the University of Hawai'i at Mānoa. I loved living there, but my ignorance of Native Hawaiian knowledge and values strained my ability to adapt. I was asked to leave by Native Hawaiian colleagues in both general and specific ways. It felt difficult to navigate and at times, unfriendly. I stayed for two years and then was lured by another faculty job.

In both Vanuatu and Hawai'i, I ultimately feel like I left prematurely for different reasons. In both cases, I could have benefited from holding steady and waiting to see what the next learning cue would be. In all of these tourist/traveler/researcher experiences, I entered without much thought about cognitive difficulty and ways to grow in my racial consciousness. Upon reflection, growth has not occurred without hardship, combined with a commitment to evolve in my singular, narrow, and limited vision through a White lens with vast global access to resources, experiences, and knowledge. Even if I left those places too early, they did not soon leave me. Even as I write this book, I have a picture of my host family from Vanuatu on the table. The things I learned in Hawai'i are not in the past tense; they are actively growing inside of me. Every day I learn new ways to short circuit the White and Western constructs in my own view of the world so that I can not only value Indigenous knowledges and epistemologies, but also crave Black ingenuity and brilliance like water in an interdependent ecosystem.

Christopher B. Newman

I was born and raised in Los Angeles, California. I grew up in the predominantly Black Leimert Park neighborhood in Los Angeles. My educational experiences were very influential on my own identity. I had all Black teachers from first through eighth grade, and my teachers placed an emphasis on important Black historical figures all year long, not just during Black History Month. I had upwards of 90 percent Black classmates. I went to an all-Black Baptist church. So, my identity was really formed around positive affirmations of being Black.

One of my first experiences with dissonance around race was in 1992 with the Los Angeles Police Department's beating of Rodney King. For one of the first times, police were caught on camera using excessive force. I remember conversations with my dad about this case, and he predicted months before the verdict was rendered that the cops would be found not guilty. "There's no way they're going to be acquitted!" I exclaimed. "Well son, I've seen this happen before, and they could have video; it doesn't matter. The trial is out in the Simi Valley. There's going to be an all-White jury. I'm guaranteeing a not guilty verdict." My dad was speaking from his many decades of experience of being Black in Los Angeles through the tumultuous 1960s; he was right.

FIGURE 2 Eating at Mzoli's in South Africa. (Photo by author.)

The five-day period starting April 29, 1992, was one of the most difficult experiences of my life. I felt like I was in the middle of a forest fire and war zone; ashes fell from the sky. I remember hearing the first police and fire engine sirens roaring near my house. It was just a surreal experience for me. I began to have a deep disdain for police and the Asian American community, because with the absence of any alternative narratives, the anti-Black sentiment and community feelings prevailed. There was a built-up tension and animosity in the Los Angeles Black community because of friction with the Asian American community who owned liquor stores throughout predominantly Black neighborhoods. The prevailing sentiment was that they were extracting financial resources and delivering poison through alcohol and tobacco products. Additionally, the narrative was that African Americans were rarely hired to work in these businesses. There were incidents of shop owners following customers around, demanding that they buy something or leave the store—all with an implied assumption of shoplifting. Infamously, Latasha Harlins was murdered by an Asian American liquor store owner, and this too was captured on video. Although convicted of voluntary manslaughter, the shop owner was sentenced only to time served and probation.

In 1994, I graduated from the eighth grade and I was fortunate enough to be accepted into Loyola High School, but it was predominantly White. It was approximately 60 percent White, 10 percent Black, 10 percent Latino, and 10 percent other racial categories. I still remember the very unsettling experience of being on the freshman football team, which started practicing a few weeks before school started. One of my new White teammates came up to me and said, "Newman, your hair is so nappy." This was my first experience being racialized and the target of racial animus. It was the first experience, but it was not the last. While in my tenth-grade year at Loyola, there was the O. J. Simpson trial. There has been renewed interest recently in the case because of the acclaim garnered by the recent FX miniseries, *The People v. O.J. Simpson: American Crime Story*. Although the series did a good job of capturing the racial divide, it did not fully capture how truly toxic racial relations were in Los Angeles at the time, a mere five years after the 1992 uprising.

Just imagine this: I was in my tenth grade Western Civilization class, and Father O'Neil, an Irish Jesuit priest, was teaching the course. There was an announcement made on the PA system that the O. J. Simpson verdict was going to be read shortly. So, we had the big tube TVs on the carts and Father O'Neil rolled out the TV, plugged it in, and tuned in to the local news channel. I am in a mostly White class of 25, maybe with one or two people of color. I remember the verdict being read and celebrating, jumping. "Yes! Not guilty." I received awful looks from my classmates and the teacher. I was thinking to myself that this is what it feels like. These two incidents, the Rodney King beating and the O. J. Simpson trial, were the nexus that accelerated my process toward making sense of my racial identity and what it means to be Black in the United States.

I have only identified as Black because in the U.S. context, until recently, one drop of Black and you are Black. All my light-skinned relatives, including my grandmother and my mother, are likely more "White" than I am, but they always identified only as Black. This however is not the case in Brazil, which has a much longer history of miscegenation and legal interracial relationships. When I travel to Brazil, I blend right in because I look mixed-race. I look Afro Brazilian. People come up to me and speak to me in Portuguese, but they quickly figure out that I am "American" when I cannot coherently respond. On two separate occasions, I traveled to Brazil as the lead faculty member with 12–18 students, and everyone pointed to me when it was time to pay the bill. Therefore, I was attributed prominence because I was perceived to have high socioeconomic status. Moreover, due to my phenotype being fairly light-skinned, I am typically treated well in Brazil. From my experience, it was very clear that Whiteness brought status and privilege that were masked within national identity. When I would subtly ask people how they identified, whether Afro Brazilian or White, they would respond, "Brazilian." Moreover, if probed long enough, some Afro Brazilians would claim African ancestry, and Afro Brazilians who are more in touch with the African diaspora would proclaim their African heritage with little prompting.

Whiteness, on the other hand, was also concealed, in that there was an assumption among those whom I was able to interact with that they were White. Many of the social challenges were not attributed to race but to socioeconomic status. Whites would attribute the relative lack of success of Afro Brazilians to social class and not to race. Any amateur ethnographer could see that Whiteness was associated with higher economic status and Blackness was attributed to lower economic status. For example, in my many visits to restaurants and mainstream shopping locales like the Rio Sul Mall in Rio de Janeiro, anyone who was handling money was White. Employees in customer service positions in a restaurant, such as servers, were White. Those engaging in more menial labor like cooking and cleaning were likely to be Afro Brazilian. When you walked past newsstands and looked at the magazine racks, you found Glamor, Cosmopolitan, and Vogue, all Brazilian editions, and all the cover models typically had White skin and straight hair. The words of Frantz Fanon reverberated in my head as he perceptively stated, "In the colonies the economic infrastructure is also a superstructure. The cause is effect: You are rich because you are white, you are white because you are rich."[1]

While Whiteness certainly is a component of economic dominance, there is a rewriting of race that intrigued me. The beauty of Brazil is that it prominently dispels how race was socially constructed for me, which was, you are either Black or you are not, or you are White or you are not. There was no gradation. Growing up, I often scoffed at those who identified as mixed-race because I felt like they were trying to separate themselves from the African diaspora to be more adjacent to Whiteness. Peter Berger in *The Social Construction of Reality* indicates that once the routine is set, habits lead to the legitimacy of the socially constructed reality. When there is a competing definition of reality, the dominant social construction of reality can only do one of two things with the competing definition: it has to annihilate it or assimilate it.

In contrast to my experiences in Brazil, I felt a great sense of angst when thinking about traveling to the African continent. I never thought I would have the opportunity to touch the continent of Africa. I grew up feeling displaced from Africa. I learned about the African diaspora at UCSB. We talk in this book about a White diaspora, which is fundamentally different than an African diaspora. The African diaspora focuses on our forceful separation from the African continent and the division that has been sowed. In spite of this, the African diaspora leads to our unity and recognition that we are one people. Nonetheless, entering South Africa, I was scared that while I had that perception of the African diaspora, Black South Africans were not going to have the same perception of me. I was anxious that I would be treated as an American—even worse, as a White American. Prior to any significant international travel, national identity was not salient for me. But in the context of South Africa, I went there worried that Black South Africans were not going to consider me to be part of the African diaspora. I remember asking a South African colleague, who self-identified as Black, "How would you identify me?" She said, "Black; we are brothers and sisters." We embraced and it was a very touching moment. It was such a powerful experience because it brought the African diaspora full circle from it being some theoretical thing that I learned about in Black studies at UCSB, to something that I actually experienced. We as a "Black race" are one people. We have been disconnected, but we are now reconnected.

Alexander Jun

I am coming into greater awareness of my light-skinned and blue passport privilege and my complicity in anti-Blackness and colorism by what I have done, as well as what I have not done. As an Asian American living in the United States I represent both the perpetrator and victim of racism. When I travel outside the United States, where I have worked and lived, I am rarely viewed as an American even though I was born just a stone's throw away from the nation's capital, Washington, D.C. Living in the United States has led me to contend with the invisibility I have experienced as an ethnic minority who is either lauded for being a model minority on the one hand, or vilified as a disease-carrying perpetual foreigner on the other. Never American enough. Never considered normal. Never treated equitably.

Living in different countries in Asia, including South Korea, I grew increasingly aware of what invisibility felt like in a positive way when I blended in physically with the dominant group. I recognized the power that comes with the association of dominant group status. I am complicit in passive acts of racism, xenophobia, and anti-Blackness that run deep in Asian countries; I am in collusion through my silence. I have also witnessed and experienced the soft power of Whiteness among some Asian nations. I am balancing this emerging awareness of privilege while simultaneously recovering from years of racialized trauma as a minority in a White dominant context in the United States. In all my travels I regularly ask host friends in Australia, New Zealand, and South Africa how I might be categorized racially in their country, and the responses are noteworthy. In Australia I was viewed at times simply as Korean by some or as culturally and linguistically diverse (CALD) by others. In South Africa my identity vacillated from White to Colored to Chinese. Most of the colleagues in New Zealand were simply not sure "what I was," but I was introduced to the new moniker Kowi (Korean Kiwi) to identify myself.

My first introduction to soft power in educational research came during my PhD program. My thesis advisor told me, "Here's a topic that I think would be good for you to pursue, and it's college mobility of first-generation Latinx students." My eyes just went blank. I'm like, "Why would I want to write about that?" And he said, "That's where the money is. There's a grant

FIGURE 3 Eating street food in Gugulethu, South Africa. (Photo by author.)

that's coming here from a foundation. This would be great for you to pursue. This is the direction that everyone's going in terms of scholarship, so you should do it." So, for me it was a very practical, personal—selfish is probably the better word—reason why I ended up pursuing research on Latinx student mobility. Interest convergence was a major factor in my decision to research a topic that was increasingly popular, with the benefit of funding attached to the research. My own tendency is to lean toward Whiteness, as I have been socialized in the United States to believe that proximity to Whiteness is tantamount to obtaining power. My own assimilationist mentality to act White is in daily conflict with cultural values that have been ingrained in me through generations. I carry a lot of the cultural assumptions and epistemologies passed down to me through my ancestors to think collectivistically and sacrifice self for community. I confess that one can take Alex out of Korea yet never take Korea out of Alex.

My proximity to Whiteness helps me when I travel to different regions of the world. For example, I had on one occasion visited a White South African chiropractor. He was treating me for back pain, and we started discussing politics. He began to talk about "all the monkeys that have taken over the country." I was surprised that he was so openly racist. It made me wonder if he assumed that I would agree with his perspective on race. Was it because of my light skin? In the eyes of this White South African, this Afrikaner, did he see me as the same? Is this what it means for me to have light-skin privilege.

My previous experiences with proximity to Whiteness taught me to say nothing to the chiropractor, not only because he was healing my lower back, but also because I learned how silence has helped me enjoy privilege. I realized it is that easy, this complicity of doing absolutely nothing because I am getting my back treated. I could offer dozens of different justifications for why I did not say anything, but it was fascinating to me. As much as I say that I am a victim of racism in the United States, I am also very much a perpetuator of racism and anti-Blackness.

My own assumptions about what New Zealand and Australia would be like reveal much about what is perpetuated both in media as well as my own mind. I assumed that being from New Zealand meant being White, being Kiwi meant being White, and being Aussie meant being White. Many of my assumptions were challenged as soon as I arrived in Sydney and Auckland, respectively. I was pleasantly surprised to encounter an overwhelming visible representation of Asians, East Asians, South Asians, and Indians. Asian restaurants owned and operated by Asian Australians were seemingly everywhere; I even saw vending machines that sold Ichiban ramen noodle cups and Pocari Sweat soft drinks. I felt at ease at the initial thought of living in these cities because I knew I would at least have my food, culture, and people represented.

As I enjoyed the comforts that came with representation, I also found myself complicit once again as I failed to recognize indigeneity, the Māori, and other disenfranchised groups in Australia and New Zealand. I failed to recognize the people who are indeed continuing to suffer at the hands of colonization, and I failed to recognize the White supremacy that is embedded in Australia and New Zealand. It was fascinating to me to observe a graduation ceremony at the University of Sydney in Australia. The graduate ceremonies had all the pomp and circumstance of a European dominant culture passed onto Australia, and almost all the graduates were from China and India.

We were in the Great Hall, which people describe as being like Hogwarts as it feels like a scene from a Harry Potter movie. I have never seen such a blatant display of overt hegemony of power over Asian people. Asians dressed up in European regalia to signify that they had "made it," and their validated educational accomplishments smacked of the colonization of the mind, while in the backdrop I saw a contested statue of William Wentworth on full display.

This experience was quite similar to what I witnessed at Curtin University in Perth, Australia. I served as a scholar in residence in the spring of 2016. One of my doctoral students conducted his dissertation research on narrative tales of Whiteness in Australia. The overwhelming majority of students in the business school were international students from Asian nations. In Perth I interacted with the national director for race and equity and tertiary education. She shared with me how the international students from China and Taiwan, and some from India, had been saving tertiary institutions financially for decades. While most were glad they could come to study, they were happier that many would return home upon completion of their degrees.

I am reminded often of the liminality of my own identity whenever I travel outside of non-Asian regions. How I am perceived by others changes based on geographic region, the histories and experiences associated with Asian people, and the curriculums and instruction on ethnic identity at all levels of education. While I have become accustomed to code-switching in the United States, I realize that this continues to be true in an ever-evolving global world. Whiteness continues to benefit from soft power, and the blue passports of the United States are at once coveted and despised, and I represent different categories to different people at different times.

Collective Lens

Though we occupy similar and different identities, the way we are perceived around the world is an entry point into this work. We strive for a collective lens, but we are not uniform. Through our many experiences with universities around the world, we find these institutions to be machines that "actualize the imperialist dreams of a settled world."[2] Stark realities like this, for us, are neither nihilistic nor deterministic. Within these colonial machines, we find the spaces for resistance. Though colonial models have been diffused around the world, the nature of that diffusion is important for developing resistance. By tracking that colonial and supremacist structure, we recognize that which came before and that which we hope will come after.

"Colonial schools carry decolonial riders."[3]

Global White Supremacy

Introduction

> We have a map of the trafficking of colonial technologies in radically different lands.[1]
> —la paperson

Knowledge is codified not only in books, but also in images, artwork, and even statues. The formal production of knowledge is uniquely tied to power through empire, belief systems, state sanctioned churches, monasteries, banks, and economy. A modern university evokes images of brick and mortar, classrooms, and student organizations. The term university is derived from a Latin phrase meaning "community of teachers and scholars." The purpose of this project is to examine ecosystems of knowledge more broadly than the boundaries of the Western university model and its claim to be the dominant—or only—rigorous house of knowledge. Indigenous knowledges and interdependence with the land sustained the vast majority of humans throughout history; but these ways of knowing were quickly disregarded within a few hundred years of discovery by European colonizers through invasion, destruction, enslavement, enlightenment, science, democracy, and industry.

Because knowledge exists everywhere, our focus on the university is not confined to campuses and classrooms. In the former colonies of Europe (e.g., South Africa, Brazil, and Oceania), contemporary universities are conflicted carriers of White dominance. Even in the curriculums, statues, architectures, language of instruction, and codes of conduct, the university stands at the clash of maintenance by empires and the cultures they invaded. The structure of the university was an institutionalization of the doctrine of discovery and its shadow side—destruction of the systems that preceded it. The imperial instinct of knowledge production was to take something in existence, then name it and claim it—a routine that exists in contemporary knowledge canons and credentials.

Structures and signals of knowledge and power are essential to our lens. In New Orleans, Louisiana, in the United States, a long, arduous, and at times violent conflict took place to remove the White supremacist statues of Civil War figures who fought to maintain the ability of states to enslave people. The endeavor included people being terrorized for working toward the removal and construction companies withdrawing their bids to complete the job. Once the statue of Confederate General Robert E. Lee was removed, the mayor of the city, Mitch Landrieu, gave a speech and later tweeted: "These statues are not just stone and metal. They are not just innocent remembrances of a benign history. These monuments purposefully celebrate a fictional, sanitized Confederacy; ignoring the death, ignoring the enslavement, and the terror that it actually stood for."[2] Around the world, the battle to maintain, establish, or remove monuments continues, and it highlights the ways in which structures of knowledge are also political weapons.

This contemporary byproduct of the clash between discovery and destruction and the erasure of existing knowledges is occurring around the world. For example, students in South Africa rallied in a protest called "Rhodes Must Fall," as depicted on the front cover of the book and in figure 4. It was a powerful movement inspired by students in 2015 when the representation of the imperialist steel magnate Cecil John Rhodes was removed from the center of the University of Cape Town. It reflects an ongoing issue around the world regarding monuments to people who represent White supremacy and its global reach. The monuments, in our view, are not just images but also imprints and ideologies. Even when the images are removed, the roots of the ideologies remain, as does the damage from the imprints.

We followed the unfolding situation as Rhodes fell, and we support the idea that "they all must fall." The irony is that just above the University of Cape Town is a monument and statue much larger than the statue that was removed from the center of the campus. Throughout the book, the monuments are a thread that highlights imprints and ideology as well as a debate about history and erasure. The argument that statue removal is a form of erasing part of history does not hold up very well. Somehow Adolf Hitler, Joseph Stalin, and Idi Amin do not require statues in order to remember their roles in history.

The trajectory of global White supremacy is deeply historical and contemporary. White terrorism reminded New Zealand of the sleeping giant of racial supremacy with a massacre on a mosque in 2019; South Africa's White minority continues to dominate in land and wealth ownership (e.g., White land ownership is over seventy percent for just ten percent of the population); and Brazil continues to struggle to find concrete ways to define race and the ways in which it operates as a proxy of privilege. How did global and social relationships

FIGURE 4 The place where Rhodes fell. (Photo by author.)

arrive at this point, and how do the history of empire and the function of universities contribute toward this contentious moment in history?

In order to comprehend these contemporary movements, modern protests, and calls for statue removals, it is critical for educators to understand the unique and tenacious spirit of conquest that has characterized the last five hundred years. White supremacy is a global, transnational, and imperial phenomenon. It has been widely transmitted through time and space in ways

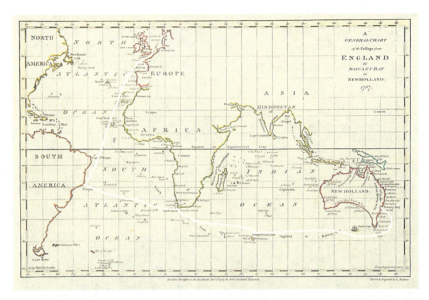

FIGURE 5 First Fleet route to Botany Bay 1787–1788 by artist John Andrews, in William Eden Auckland's *History of New Holland, from its First Discovery in 1616 to the Present Time*. State Library of New South Wales.

that are often difficult to name. The fruits of Whiteness that emerged from the fertile soils of Europe produced a now centuries-long stretch of dominance. The way humanity changed starting in 1500 CE, produced an extreme kind of growth that someone living prior to that time period would not be able to fathom. During that stretch of history, a global conquest for empire and the quest for knowledge through a scientific revolution produced drastically altered social arrangements. The movements also deposited colonial settlements with White ideologies and systems all over the globe.

One particular voyage departing from Europe in 1787 captures the idea of a White homeland both sending and establishing White diasporas in the Global South through a variety of means. A set of ships called the First Fleet embarked from England to settle in Botany Bay, Australia. Along the way they stopped in Rio de Janeiro, Brazil, and Cape Town, South Africa, before proceeding to Botany Bay. Each of these stops is located on the 1787 map in figure 5, and they represent the three regions of this study. These three regions embodied long histories of culture, belief, and interdependence with the natural environment. Upon interaction with European settlers, they came to exemplify a construction of colorism and racialization that happened across time and space. The connections between the way Europe (and later North America) categorized and codified people, culture, and knowledge became a type of epistemicide, which is the way in which discovery and destruction became two sides of the same initiative that wiped out particular ways of knowing. Settler colonialism is an antecedent for what we know as a global White supremacy and anti-Blackness. Those terms articulate the poles on the spectrum of racism, and the role of knowledge production and its relationship to the university help to preserve a violent and distorted view of the world through a racialized lens that masqueraded as discovery and contact. Everything after "contact" became knowledge in the university canon, and everything that came before it was the subject of dispassionate academic inquiry, which is a colonial capsule of the powerful first knowledges and cultures that preceded the gaze of the settler. We move from examining the invasion of the settlers to the colonizing function of universities.

Ghosts and Skeletons

We traverse across time and geography because we are chasing ghosts. This project is not limited to a historical reflection, but those roots help us grasp the fruits exhibited in contemporary violence. Our study is not an isolated analysis of the contemporary because the often-unseen origins of the violence are nearby. Avery F. Gordon describes the appearance of ghosts as a way to explain that which has been concealed but is very much alive, present, and interfering to produce a haunting and ceaseless repression. The haunting describes the "repressed or unresolved social violence [that] is making itself known, sometimes very directly, sometimes more obliquely."[3] There are many paradigms through which to understand the lengthy history of settler colonial violence, and we use multiple metaphors along the way to confront the complexity. A linear view of time prevents a deep understanding; but in the context of colonial violence as the precursor for racialized violence, we draw from Linda Tuhiwai Smith and la paperson in acknowledging that schools and universities are running on paradoxical desires for the colonizer's future and Indigenous futures in that colonization is now, the preceding time was precolonial, and the future is decolonial.[4]

To transcend the time, paradox, and complexity, the idea of a haunting provides the framework for understanding that the ghost is the signal that the haunting is taking place. The ghost is not an individual or an identity but rather a social figure or even a structure; and any inquiry into it leads to a deep history, context, and compounding set of byproducts by which it can be understood. Analyzing hauntings can lead to a more complex perspective on the "generative structures and moving parts of historically embedded social formations."[5] Our investigation is multicontextual and multifaceted in that it is both the rigid and limited social science we were trained in, but also a conjuring of the things our training and acculturation have not given us eyes to see. We are chasing ghosts—inside us and all around us.

When starting with terms like White supremacy, we can quickly get lost in the limited context of the contemporary view. Settler colonialism is the generative context for racism, which in turn created the untidy concept of race.[6] We do not intend to settle the debate on the origin of the concept of race. It is akin to attempting a start date for the origin of a species that is ever evolving. However, the settler colonial pursuit of land generated and sustained a certain type of violence:

> Settlers arrive in a new (to them) place and claim it as theirs. They destroy and then later erase (via assimilation or cultural strangling) Indigenous peoples, and use weapons and policy to extinguish their/our claims to land. Settlement requires the labor of chattel slaves and guest workers, who must be kept landless and estranged from their homelands... Inquiry as invasion is a result of the imperative to produce settler colonial knowledge and to produce it for the academy. This invasion imperative is often disguised in universalist terms of producing "objective knowledge" for "the public."[7]

What emerges, then, are constructs such as property law. In violently separating people from the land, the settler machinery creates a divorce from ways of knowing, being, and living. Instead of an interdependent relationship with the land, the paper signifying ownership takes precedent. Then manipulation of land as a resource through the plow and the bulldozer sustains a tacit view of hierarchy in nature. Property law is a settler colonial tool, as are the "weapons to enforce it, the knowledge institutions that legitimize it, [and] the financial institutions that operationalize it."[8]

Notions of superiority grow, travel, and mutate.[9] These ideologies spread and take root in different soils and then become hybridized versions of the social organism that preceded the contemporary form. In this way, the settler, not as identity but as social structure or form, is the context from which White supremacy emerges. These traveling notions and tools of settler colonialism in the past and present connect the haunting of how anti-Blackness became a global project. The opposite ends of the colorism spectrum require symbolic opposites in order to sustain the top side of the hierarchy. A settler is a position of allowance from which Whiteness emerges: "Whiteness is property; it is the right to have rights; it is the legal human."[10] Willie Jennings adds masculinity and self-sufficiency to Whiteness, which is defined not as a person or people, but rather a way of organizing a logic system. Whiteness, then, does not refer to people of European descent but to a "way of being in the world and seeing the world that forms cognitive and affective structures able to seduce people into its habitation and its meaning making."[11]

Whiteness and supremacy cannot be sustained without the construction of inferiority, generating the ideology of anti-Blackness. The assault on Indigenous land and the transformation of people as chattel uphold a spectrum that has been revealed in many ways. The expansion of settler colonialism turned White supremacy became the haunting of centuries. The tools, mutations, and transportations make it hard to track down at times, but in conjuring these tools, we approach the task with inspiration and purpose: to "wreck, scavenge, retool, and reassemble the colonizing university into decolonizing contraptions."[12] We chase ghosts, conjure the hauntings, and map the journey of mutation with decolonizing desires.

Strands of History

Throughout human history, there have been a few forces that have not only created the foundation of the way our modern society works but have become *tools* of invasion (described more fully in chapter 1). The strands that have bound human cooperation from the earliest formations include belief systems, the exchange of goods/currency, empire, and knowledge.[13]

The first strand that tied society together is that of shared beliefs. Whether norms, values, or religions, extensive shared beliefs become superhuman either through an identified god or a superordinate identity that has godlike powers in a society. Belief systems take on a variety of characteristics, but one common distinction throughout history has been between polytheism and monotheism. Polytheism is a broad term for a faith or belief in many gods, some of whom may be in competition with each other. Hinduism, Greco-Roman religion, and Buddhism are examples of this form of religion. Conversely, the belief in a one-and-only God led some people to believe that they were in possession of a singular truth, which gave way to instances of a more fanatical and proselytizing disposition. Distinct from the otherworldly nature of monotheism, there is also a type of worship of humanity with the belief that humans can either evolve or devolve. Efforts at social evolution created godlike qualities for some while conversely implementing subhuman characteristics for others.

The second strand to bind humanity together is rooted in an economy, which came to operate through currency and eventually capitalism. Currency can convert anything into money as long as there is trust and cooperation that the coinage can be used to represent value. This is an ancient practice that has continued to evolve. The dominant economic system of the last few centuries has arguably been capitalism, which is a further extension of that trust. This system requires faith in the cooperating party, but also a profound trust in future growth. It is built upon the assumption that the pool of resources is ever expanding, and faith in the future size of that pool of resources allows for an immediate operating beyond the proximate means. Trade and trust led to a level of global unification that had not been experienced in the bulk of human history.

The third strand of a more global order is that of empire. Societies throughout history have tried to expand borders with a desire for growth. When a conqueror/colonizer takes over another localized society, that society has to be incorporated into the larger empire through assimilation or else annihilated and retained only for land and resources.[14] If the strands of belief (religions), trade (economy), and empire equated to a period of global convergence and unification, then knowledge systems from localized, animistic, hunting and foraging, Indigenous cultures were all disenfranchised and/or eradicated by the unified global system.

The fourth and final strand that serves to cement global orders of unification through empire, money, and beliefs is that of knowledge codified into science. From the Renaissance in the mid-1500s to the following centuries of Enlightenment and our contemporary knowledge production setting, the knowledge system emerging from Europe and bridging to North America has been a scientific revolution. Many religions (both polytheistic and monotheistic) claim that everything known or that needs to be known can be found in a sacred text. Science, however, is based on an assumption of ignorance—that is, humans do not know everything, which means there is knowledge to gain, acquire, and discover. Furthermore, through observation, repetition, rigor, and analysis (known as research), discoveries can create knowledge, which can create power.

Each singular strand represented a major disruption on a global scale, but the weaving of these strands constituted an entire new order of humanity. The relationship among ideologies to justify the search for new knowledge, the capital to fund the search for knowledge, and the acquisition of new land, natural resources, and people through empire, constitutes a cycle of power that has been the dominant world order for the last five centuries.[15]

The roles of settler colonialism, race, geography, invasion, homelands, diasporas, and universities are topics in this book that build upon a world order of unification, power, and knowledge. If the bulk of human history is about localized societies and their interdependent relationship with the land, the most recent five hundred years has been about rapid expansion with a dominant/dependent relationship with the land. The explorers who are given credit in history books for "discovering" new lands set sail on dangerous expeditions looking for resources to support depressed economies in the homeland, places to claim for their respective crowns, and new knowledge. This last point about knowledge, however, is not often captured adequately in historical narratives, because it has such variable application.

Consider the example of Captain James Cook (1728–1779)—a famous figure in historical accounts of invasion in the name of exploration. The Royal Society, committed to the improvement of natural knowledge, helped fund his expeditions, and the Royal Navy provided ships and protection. There were many scientists aboard the expeditions, collecting information about geography, botany, astronomy, weather patterns, and cultures. At each destination the ships landed (e.g., Australia, New Zealand, etc.), they planted a seed of invasion. Those seeds were rooted in a European occupation and the establishment of a White diaspora—a White settlement distant and distinct from the homeland of Europe. Because the acts of conquest in the name of exploration took place on a quest for knowledge, conquest under the banner of exploration represented a contribution to global unification under an empire. The byproduct was the near genocide of the localized cultures of the first peoples who were already inhabiting the land. Native populations that survived were then subjected to some version of religious ideology and racial science that forced them to assimilate or suffer a slower version of annihilation. A statue of Cook is still prominently placed in Christchurch, New Zealand.

Yuval Harari summarizes a cohesive theory of that which cemented the bond between modern science and imperialism emerging from Europe, and it was the mindset of conquest.[16] A strong appetite for new knowledge and new territory was aptly illustrated by the occupations of many of those traveling on ships to distant lands: naval officers and botanists. From Napoleon invading Egypt in 1798 with an army and a huge team of scientists, to the Royal Navy's conquest of South America with Charles Darwin on board, acquisition of land and knowledge became almost synonymous. As data was collected, domination was enacted. More knowledge about culture, history, linguistics, biology, and climate created recipes for successful invasion. Religion played an ambivalent role in that many thought God was being eliminated in some ways by science. However, the monotheistic fervor for proselytizing remained a useful ideology for invasion and conquest. Religion was not replaced but rather syncretized with empire and science. Religion no longer provided the answers, but it was an effective tool for cultivating belief and justifying invasion so as to civilize and save those labeled as "barbaric" peoples. Science did not eliminate God; rather, it replaced God with scientists and kept religion as a vehicle for enacting empire. In that powerful cycle, science fed empires with the belief in superiority and human progress.

Rudyard Kipling's 1899 poem captures the ideology, spirit, and appetite for invasion. It was written at a time when he was encouraging the occupation of the Philippines.

> Take up the White Man's burden—
> Send forth the best ye breed—
> Go send your sons to exile
> To serve your captives' need
> To wait in heavy harness
> On fluttered folk and wild—

> Your new-caught, sullen peoples,
> Half devil and half child
> Take up the White Man's burden
> In patience to abide
> To veil the threat of terror
> And check the show of pride;
> By open speech and simple
> An hundred times made plain
> To seek another's profit
> And work another's gain
> Take up the White Man's burden—

Across Southern Africa, Brazil/South America, and Australia/New Zealand/Oceania there were litanies of conquests that connected the globe through empire. The religious and scientific ideologies with capitalist financiers were powerful connections. Linguists and the belief that all European languages descended from Sanskrit peoples who called themselves Arya provided a foundation to link evolutionary biology in promoting a belief in a "pure race" called Aryans. Those who intermixed with Indigenous peoples from various lands around the world lost their purity, but European Aryans sought to preserve the race (and thus their superiority/supremacy) by not mixing with inferior races. Race, science, religion, empire, and economy cannot be separated. Harari suggests, "There are very few scientific disciplines that did not begin their lives as servants to imperial growth and do not owe a large portion of their discoveries, collections, buildings and scholarships to the generous help of army officers, navy captains and imperial governors."[17] The diligent gardeners of this systematic knowledge, as both codifiers and disseminators, are universities. The universities that educated the scientists and that deposited people and ideas all over the world were replicated in those distant lands. As the people syncretized their culture and tried to justify their existence and robustness to the White homelands of Europe, their tenacity and desire to succeed combined with an underdog mentality to form a White diaspora. The White diaspora was created by the seeds of the White homeland; but in different soil and conditions, it grew into different beings. Though the universities in the diaspora were filled with professors from the homeland and modeled everything from architecture to curriculum, the culture and the universities evolved as hybrids.

An imperialist invader with all the knowledge and power of the homeland who developed a victim mentality and who was longing for home or justification (or both), emerged as a uniquely dangerous colonizer. Figure 6 is a photo we took of an image in Zambia with the caption "The Double Face of Colonialism," which is taken to mean violence and religion because of the gun and the Bible held by the figure in the picture.

FIGURE 6 Image from a museum in Zambia. (Photo by author, artwork by Milliot Ngoma and titled *The Double Face of Colonialism*. Used with permission by the Livingstone Museum.)

By adding the roles of economy and knowledge/education, we see more of the haunting. It is a hegemony that exists throughout society that prevents epistemological access to education. By codifying knowledge and creating a hierarchy, the knowledge held by the Indigenous peoples before invasions is disenfranchised. In our decolonizing pursuits, we understand that "there must be cognitive justice before there can be social justice."[18]

Preview of the Chapters

The book is divided into two parts: ideology and case studies. The purpose of the first part is to examine settler colonialism as a multiplicity of tools in the service of White supremacy. Of principal importance are the ways of knowing that have been produced and expressed in social relationships, family history, caring for the land, and many other ways throughout the history of human society. In Europe (and later in North America), the movement to codify knowledge in more rigid, linear, and binary ways emerged and became a globalized system of higher education. Universities, in the modern and Western form, now occupy the center of knowledge production and certification (research and issuing diplomas).

The second part of the book is an exploration of the Southern Hemisphere, some of which represents the Global South. The Global South is not as simplistic or rigid as the Southern Hemisphere, though much of it resides there. It is a geopolitical location. Santos locates the Global South through a series of questions: "What is there in the South that escapes the North/South dichotomy? What is there in traditional medicine that escapes the modern medicine/traditional medicine dichotomy? What is there in woman, apart from her relation with man? Is it possible to see the subaltern regardless of the relation of subalternity? Could it be possible that the countries considered less developed are more developed in fields that escape the hegemonic terms of dichotomy?"[19] In this way, that which is the geopolitical location of the Global North is not comprehensible without a symbolic relationship with the Global South. This is similar to the ways in which traditional knowledge is not intelligible outside its relation to scientific knowledge or Black outside relation to White. The symbolic opposites and poles of the spectrum provide meaning, function, and hierarchy to social relationships and structures.

Through our travels to South America (primarily Brazil, but also Argentina and Venezuela), Southern Africa (primarily South Africa, but also Zambia and Zimbabwe), and Oceania (primarily Australia and New Zealand, but also Vanuatu), we started with the contemporary university and worked our way around, under, behind, and before in search of ghosts. With a commitment to decolonizing the tools at work both in and outside of us, we became students of the knowledges that predate and have survived the settler colonial invasion and the universities that carry and maintain those tools.

Part I: Ideology

Chapter 1: Tools of Invasion: A Disposition to Inhabit the Globe. Like much of this introductory chapter, the tools of invasion are a continuation of the line of thinking around global unifiers in human history. Moving from the conceptualization as strands within human history, this chapter turns to focus on how they come together in various combinations as tools of invasion. The concept of a tool elicits imagery of both function and impact—something generative to produce a chain reaction or ripple effect. The tools work together through varying configurations to produce different effects in different regions and cultures in the world, but the core or purpose of the tools remains—that of invasion. Religion, economy, empire, and science come together as a flexible and mutable concoction to produce long-term, insidious, and haunting results. The core of all these combinations is the settler colonial appetite for conquest.

Chapter 2: Homeland, Diaspora, and Traveling Whiteness. The notion of a diaspora is a community that exists in physical (and perhaps emotional, spiritual, or cultural) distance from a homeland. For example, Jewish diasporas exist at some distance from Israel, and Black/African diasporas exist away from homelands on the African continent. The homeland represents the origin and development of an identity, and the diaspora represents some struggle to maintain or redefine that identity in light of disruption and distance. During the history of colonial settlements expanding out of the European homeland, White diasporas emerged around the world. This concept moves beyond that of a colonial outpost to looking more deeply at the ways in which White identity developed and evolved away from the homeland of Europe. Simultaneously, the White diasporas disrupted the Indigenous homelands around the globe and created a tear in the interdependent fabric of people and their relationship with the land. As the White diasporas caused disruption, Indigenous diasporas were created all over the globe as people became chattel and property. Both sides of this phenomenon create the context for understanding the transition from settler colonialism to White supremacy around the world.

Chapter 3: The University as Colonizer and Carrier of White Dominance. Religious structures (temples, monasteries, churches, mosques, etc.) have been centers of meaning and knowledge production throughout history. For example, monasteries in many regions supported the production of agriculture, crafts, books, art, and philosophies as the core of producing and maintaining knowledge and identity. For hundreds of years, colleges and universities came alongside religious structures and operated in tandem to uphold that meaning and support the state. Some of the earliest colleges in the modern era existed to produce clergy and civil servants/leaders. The power center existed at the intersection between religion and the state. During the scientific revolution (sixteenth to eighteenth centuries), religion was destabilized and new forms of evidence challenged the notion of meaning-making with knowledge production. The codification of linear methods to generate new knowledge spread through Europe's conquest of the globe. Royal societies, colleges, and universities came together to generate new academic disciplines with a new understanding of what was acceptable knowledge in the world. The Western development of science transformed warfare, medicine, travel, government, individual and social interventions, and much more. The Enlightenment and revolutions in science and industry left the university as the center of knowledge production. Settler colonialism from Europe was the generative context for notions of White superiority, supremacy, and dominance. European (and later North American) universities were recreated in almost every region of the world. They reproduced not only the original form, structure, and architecture, but also the curriculum, methods, and epistemologies—all of which were laced with notions of racialized superiority.

Part II—Case Studies

Chapter 4: Dominant White Minorities and Invasion in Southern Africa. On the southern tip of the African continent, a variety of peoples settled and lived for tens of thousands of years prior to the arrival of European explorers, settlers, and colonizers. Following the exploitation of natural resources, the drawing of arbitrary lines to create republics, and then independence from colonial power, three countries among those where White expansion played a unique role include Zimbabwe, Zambia, and South Africa. The cape of South Africa became a point of interest to the Dutch East India Company and other traders who established supply stops on trade routes. Eventually some of the Dutch (many of whom were Calvinists who were persecuted in Europe) stayed in the region and migrated away from the cape to the inland areas and created farms there. The Dutch word for farmer is *boers*, and so the identity for many of the Dutch settlers who have been on the land for a long time is characterized by speaking Afrikaans (a derivative of the Dutch language) and going by the term Boers. The British also settled there and officially annexed the Cape Colony in the early nineteenth century, setting up a conflict between the British elite and the rugged Dutch farmers, dubbed the Anglo-Boer wars. These wars ended in the early twentieth century under a treaty to create the Union of South Africa, which included self-governing colonies of Afrikaners and others. Two settler colonial forms existed in tension: Dutch/Afrikaners and the British. The Afrikaners eventually took control through the Nationalist Party, and the architecture of apartheid was put together at Stellenbosch University. Two warring and tenacious White minorities wreaked havoc on South Africa with decades of a brutal apartheid regime—with the university at the epicenter of its thoughts and actions. In the contemporary setting, with formal apartheid over, the university is a site of contention. It has all the settler colonial residue, as well as movements by and of the people to Africanize the curriculum and create epistemological access as cognitive justice.

Chapter 5: Shades of Advantage in Brazil. For centuries, the region now known as Brazil was home to the Tupi Guarani, Arawak, Carib, and Ge, among other

Indigenous tribes. These civilizations were primarily hunters, gatherers, and farmers. The Indigenous peoples of these lands cultivated a wide variety of crops and developed preservation techniques to store harvests, which allowed their civilizations to flourish. When the Portuguese first arrived in Brazil, they established a trading port with a keen interest in many of the raw materials, including brazilwood (sappanwood), which is used to produce a natural red dye. Brazil was named after this exploitable natural resource. The Portuguese eventually colonized Brazil to defend their trade monopoly from other Europeans, such as the Dutch. Through subjugation and integration, religious conversion, and the spreading of diseases, the Portuguese took control over Brazil from the Indigenous population. The introduction of the slave economy produced an entirely unique White diaspora, even after slavery ended. With a history of miscegenation among the Portuguese, Indigenous peoples, and enslaved Africans, a durable Brazilian national identity was formed, cloaked with a White diasporic substructure. As the last country to end the enslavement of Africans, in 1888, the Brazil case examines the only Portuguese-speaking country in the Americas through the lens of the tools of invasion to unpack the distinctive ways the Portuguese established an enduring legacy of White supremacy and anti-Blackness. In 1792, the first symbolages of a higher education institution in colonial Brazil was founded as the Polytechnic School (Escola Politecnica). To perpetuate a dependence on the White homeland, the Portuguese preserved the "university" designation for the University of Coimbra, which was founded in Portugal in 1292. Well after the colonial ties to Brazil were severed, the Federal University of Rio de Janeiro (Universidade Federal do Rio de Janeiro) unified the assortment of colleges. The universities in Brazil have been at the center of political and social power struggles through access to the universities and the inclusion of a curriculum reflective of the many contributions of Afro Brazilians and Indigenous people.

Chapter 6: Empty Treaties and Occupied Land in Oceania. In Australia and the neighboring island Aotearoa (New Zealand), Indigenous peoples cultivated self-sustaining societies for thousands of years prior to European contact. The sovereign nation of Aotearoa was given the name Nova Zeelandia by Dutch cartographers in 1645. British colonizer James Cook later anglicized the name to New Zealand. As with many other clashes of cultures, what transpired over several hundred years was violence and the estrangement of an Indigenous way of life. The clash of cultures worked to establish a White normativity. The "First Fleet" that arrived in Botany Bay, Australia, brought with it all of the tools of invasion, and these neighboring islands were transformed into unique diasporas. Universities were modeled after Cambridge and Oxford, and before long a "White Australia" policy was enacted to ensure that the destruction of the Indigenous peoples would not be followed by a replacement by anyone other than those of European descent. In both places, there is persistent tension and violence around the founders of the universities and a struggle to transform them into places that do more than just acknowledge the land they occupy; there is an intense desire to rewire the learning and knowledge production environment into something that is epistemologically inclusive and recognizes the active knowledge systems that the very existence of the university served to threaten.

The End at the Beginning

We live, work, and operate in a colonized space. We are complicit. We are colonizers. It has taken a great effort to examine the core of our epistemological dispositions that exist because of our colonial training. As a result of our self-excavation, we have taken great care to examine the knowledge systems that came before settler colonialism. In doing so, our purpose and trajectory have been to recognize our position within the house of knowledges where we reside, and stand committed to decolonizing. There will be many contours of our decolonizing efforts. They will be fraught, incomplete, and compromised. Our commitment to decolonizing begins with the recognition of our own colonized minds. We seek a rematriation[20] to the land and a reimagining of what knowledges, methods, spiritualities, and cultures will be in the future. This project is both incomplete and necessary at the same time. The context, history, and perspective offered here should serve as an introduction to the disruption of the ways in which our university and academic dispositions have and continue to serve as sites of colonial and White supremacist preservation—as well as sites of resistance.

Part 1
Ideology

1

Tools of Invasion

A Disposition to Inhabit the Globe

If commerce, empire, and religion equal global unification, then knowledge systems from localized, animistic, hunting and foraging indigenous cultures were all disenfranchised and eradicated by unified and global systems.[1]

Colonial technologies travel. In tracing technologies' past and future trajectories, we can connect how settler colonial and antiblack technologies circulate in transnational arenas... The "settler" is not an identity; it is the idealized juridical space of exceptional rights granted to normative settler citizens and the idealized exceptionalism by which the settler exerts its sovereignty. The "settler" is a site of exception from which whiteness emerges. Whiteness is property; it is the right to have rights; it is the legal human.[2]

Introduction

In this chapter we present a set of intertwined tools of invasion that have been critical to settler colonial domination: religion, economy, empire, and science. At the center of those four tools is a craving for conquest. This broad cross section of tools was not used equally by every colonial power in every locale, but unique combinations of the tools shaped the varying approaches in different regions in the Southern Hemisphere in the seventeenth and eighteenth centuries. The combinations of strands eventually contributed to an altered version of Whiteness that looked different than in the homelands of Europe. While some might have relied more on religion (e.g., the Dutch Reformed Church theology in South Africa), others focused more on empire and acquisition of land and resources (e.g., Spain and Portugal in South America), and others carried scientists on their ships, making the acquisition of knowledge and hostile takeover of land two sides of the same coin (e.g., England venturing to Australia and New Zealand).

Any rope has a construction of wires and strands that are laid together to form the whole. Some ropes have a core, like the one pictured in figure 7, which represents the central component in the invasions and conquests that took place around the globe. The strands represent four of the most common tools, with the core as the driving force behind this combination. When invaders used both religion and economy, they were able to employ belief systems to colonize not only bodies (labor) but also the mind (knowledge) and spirit. Other settler initiatives started with imperial force, whereby they were only able to colonize bodies through forced labor and genocide.

The rope is made up of strands tightly woven to enhance its strength and pliability, making it a useful tool with many applications. The simplicity and broad applicability of a rope highlights the function of not only the strands and threads within the rope but also the rope as a tightly wound unit. In trying to comprehend the complexity of this multifaceted tool, we sought to examine it in an unraveled state to enhance the view of the various components. The threads and strands are the components and context of the flexible and powerful tool. In a metaphor-bending way, we also see the various fibers, threads, and strands of the rope as similar in figure to tree roots. Tree roots absorb soil, minerals, and water to generate the trunk, branches, leaves, and fruit that are visible above the ground. In a similar way, the historical roots/strands provide insights into the contemporary fruits of settler colonialism and White supremacy.

We recognize the tension in trying to describe this complex process that is not monolithic but rather incoherent and contorted, even in its power. Part of our objective is also to: "Treat as problematic the making of both colonizers and colonized in order to understand better the forces that, over time, have drawn them into an extraordinarily intricate web of relations. This goes

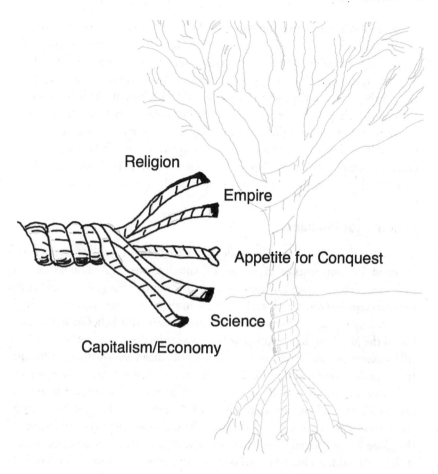

FIGURE 7 Tools of Invasion as Rope and Roots. (Illustration created by author.)

much further than to restate the commonplace that the colonizing process is characterized by occasional conflict, as well as common interests among its perpetrators—be they administrators or industrialists, merchants or militia, the crown or the cloth. To be sure, its contradictions everywhere run far deeper than are suggested by the tensions visible on the surface planes of empire."[3] The newly invaded territories were White dominant at the outset of contact, but because they were distinct from the White homelands, they became the White diaspora. The nature of the persons willing to depart from the homelands—as well as their trades, religions, dispositions, legal status, and personal interests—all shaped the new variants of what became a global White supremacy. The unique production of superiority between the homeland and the diaspora also utilized universities (both in the homeland and the newly formed in the diaspora) as incubators of White supremacy's logic and ideology.

The following sections outline various tools of invasion. It is essential to keep in mind that they are parts of an intertwined rope. When you try to untangle something so intricately woven together, it can appear more muddled than distinct. It is impossible to keep these concepts and sections completely separate, as they are interdependent in the way they illuminate the belief systems undergirding human societies. Accordingly, our attempt to dissect the rope for the purposes of greater understanding begins with the core appetite for conquest, followed by the four tools: religion, empire, science, and capitalist economy. All four of the tools overlap with the role of universities that are eventually established in the colonial sites—as well as the driving force of conquest.

Appetite for Conquest

The core of the tools of invasion model is centered in the capacity for conquest. Much of the continents of Africa, South America, parts of Asia, and Oceania were sites of conquest for European powers. The kind of imperialism that began in the sixteenth century and reached a peak in the nineteenth century was characterized by notions of superiority and civilization. This belief in superiority fueled the justification for conquests of many sorts, including military, scientific exploration, and religious. European imperialism was distinctly different from previous forms of domination in the world. It was larger in size, scope, longevity, stratification, and organization. The phrase "The sun never sets on the British Empire" characterized some of this scope; but when combined with conquests by the United States through the early twentieth century, most of the globe was impacted by colonialism. The appetite for conquest, according to Edward Said, is characterized by the culture that incubated this kind of inclination:

> At the heart of European culture during the many decades of imperial expansion lay an undeterred and unrelenting Eurocentrism. This accumulated experiences, territories, peoples, histories; it studied them, it classified them, it verified them ... it subordinated them by banishing their identities except as a lower order of being, from the culture and indeed the very idea of white Christian Europe.... This Eurocentric culture relentlessly codified and observed everything about the non-European or peripheral world, and so thoroughly and in so detailed a manner as to leave few items untouched, few cultures unstudied, few peoples and spots of land unclaimed.[4]

Though the culture was not uniform or monolithic, it shared a common colonial thread that distinguished it from other imperial pursuits. No matter the combination or depth of application of the tools applied to the expansion of empire, at the core was a relentless pursuit.

The role of knowledge production and dissemination as well as the desire to be right come into full view in the structure of settler colonial mentalities. Inquiry as a type of invasion becomes another signal of the appetite for conquest:

> Inquiry as invasion is a result of the imperative to produce settler colonial knowledge and to produce it for the academy. This invasion imperative is often disguised in universalist terms of producing "objective knowledge" for "the public." It is a thin disguise, as most research rhetoric waxes the poetics of empire: to discover, to chart new terrain, to seek new frontiers, to explore, and so on. The academy's unrelenting need to produce "original research" is what makes the inquiry an invading structure, not an event. Social science hunts for new objects of study, and its favored reaping grounds are Native, urban, poor, and Othered communities.[5]

We discuss the idea of inquiry as invasion in greater detail in chapter 3, but the eradication of Indigenous knowledge and structures of formalized education are the fruit born from the root of an unsatiable appetite for conquest. Power and identity generate normativity around race, gender, ability, class, and sexuality. The visibility of those identities varies depending on the position of power and cultural movements of their time.

The social construct of race is at the center of much of our analysis throughout the book. However, race does not stand alone as an independent identity. It is intricately intertwined with other social constructs. For example, women who were joining colonial expeditions from Europe always occupied the precarious space of being subjected to male domination but reinforcing White dominance in newly colonized spaces. White women, in some ways, made the violent pursuits of supremacy appear more innocent or showed that they were acquiescing in their own suffering through patriarchy. By denying or defending these forms of supremacy, they became essential components of the tools of invasion.

One acute example was the insidious removal of Indigenous children from their families in Australia. This well-documented atrocity also occurred in other regions of the world through the demonization of family structures and mothering. In Australia, the "colonial maternalists" used their status (both privileged over Indigenous peoples but subjugated to White men) to "simultaneously collaborate with and confound colonial aims."[6] In a similar vein, Tiffany Lethobo King identifies how the Black woman, body, womb, and mother were treated just as land was treated during settler colonialism and enslavement. The land was governed then by paper for the purposes of manipulation, extraction, production, and settlement. Black women and their bodies are metaphors as fungible units of exchange, with value and extraction surrounding even the products of their wombs.[7] The appetite for conquest is at the core of the settler mentality and does not stop at land or people. The acquisition of spirit, mind, and social organization follow suit.

Religion

The first significant strand/tool of invasion is found in the manipulation of religious texts and ideas to justify imperial action. Some religious missionaries had a deep desire to "save" groups of people from their own "barbarous ways." In the same vein they used a deity to justify their own intellectual and spiritual superiority over "the other." Definitions of salvation manifested in manifold ways, but one consistent trend was evident in all missionary endeavors: the conflation of faith with progress, enlightenment, and culture. The fruits of religious missionary endeavors have been scattered across the Global South, some of which will be explored later in the case study chapters. Religion serves many purposes but embedded in the construction and claims of belief systems, it also served as a tool of invasion.

Christianity in particular provided specific theological parameters that guided one aspect of the justification, if not the inspiration, for global conquest. Though religion has been a source of disagreement, division, and even violence, it has also been a type of unifier in human societies (along with the other tools of invasion). Social constructions, belief systems, and unifiers are fragile, and they all become harder to maintain as a society grows. Religion aided in giving legitimacy to fragile structures, thus providing a "sacred canopy" of protection in that: "Religions assert that our laws are not the result of human caprice but are ordained by an absolute and supreme authority. This helps place at least some fundamental laws beyond challenge, thereby ensuring social stability. Religion can thus be defined as a system of human norms and values that is founded on a belief in a superhuman order."[8] Polytheism characterized the belief systems of much of early human history. Judaism was monotheistic in a local way in that their depiction of God was focused on engaging with the small nation of Israel. The monotheism of Christianity, emerging from Judaism, carried a universal message of salvation for all of humanity. With the belief of possession of the truth in the one and only God, in order to sustain the absolute nature of their truth, Christians had to discredit other belief systems. A second monotheistic giant emerged in the form of Islam, which, along with Christianity, tended to be more fervent and missionary oriented than polytheistic religions.

The monotheistic claim to one God helped to produce a totality in thinking and belief that enhanced the ability to label someone or some thinking as either completely right or completely wrong. This type of reasoning and logic sanctions dualistic constructions, including saved/damned, civilized/

barbarous, capital/labor, North/South, West/East, Black/White, legal/illegal, superior/inferior, and valuable/discardable.[9] The dualism of man and woman was also essential, as women were denied access to many aspects of religious participation, creating another hierarchy that fed into the complexity of race. Medieval European society had Christianity as a root system for guiding belief, reason, logic, and action. The roots of the logic created fruits and byproducts that were far-reaching in the form of conquest.

Consider the papal bull of Pope Paul II in 1537 that declared that "Indians" (Indigenous peoples in the Americas) have a soul.[10] Through a contemporary lens this statement may be regarded as an important prohibition against the enslavement of "unknown peoples" (even though it was largely disregarded). However, pushing this designation to its logical conclusion, the declaration of possessing a soul rendered them able to be saved, thus establishing that these people are empty receptacles needing to be filled with faith or religion. This is significant because any other belief system was disregarded, and only because it was replaceable could the religious authority justify (though unsuccessfully in practice) the protection of the receptacle.

Invaders employed the banner of religion as a useful method of conversion, which, given the conflation of ideals stated earlier, meant far more than merely a conversion to a Western religion. In Christian missionary work, for example, the object of worship was "neither Jesus Christ nor his Father, God, but Western man and Western civilization."[11] The utilization of religion became a useful ruse to establish and maintain White civilization as so superior it was divine. As settler colonial invaders began expeditions, the idea that the land was empty and available (*terra nullius*) corresponded with the notion that souls needed to be taken as well (*anima nullius*). This was a violent act, because neither the land nor the humans inhabiting the land were empty; but the religious justification oriented their initiative.

Consider the lands of Egypt and Ethiopia, where the very first builders of civilization were Black. The invasion of Africa by Islam was followed by European Christianity and colonialism. In each successive invasion, the history of the birthplace of civilization was explained away by unfortunate or ill-conceived migrations, and the successes of Black civilizations have been erased through the process of what Chancellor Williams called the "Caucasianization in Egypt": "The long, long struggle to take from the Blacks whatever they had of human worth, their land and all their wealth therein, their bodies, their soul, and their minds, was a process of steady depersonalization, dehumanization."[12] The nature of anti-Blackness is fully present in the understanding of the conquest. It disregards Black intellect and spirituality, and it uses the notion of not just a higher power but the highest power to colonize the mind and spirit. Mark Mathabane in his autobiography *Kaffir Boy* depicts a Black African evangelist as saying:

"See how the devil speaks through you," the cross-eyed evangelist gloated. "Everybody needs Christ. Our forefathers, who for centuries had lived in utter darkness in the jungles of Africa, worshipping false gods involving human sacrifices, needed Christ bad. That's why God from his sacred seat in heaven one day looked at Africa and said to Himself, 'I cannot in all fairness let those black children of mine continue to follow the evil path. They've already suffered enough for the transgressions of their cursed father, Ham. I've got to save them somehow.' 'But how can I save them,' the mighty God wondered, 'for there's none among them who knows how to read or write, therefore I cannot send them my Ten Commandments.' God worried over the problem for days and nights, until one day he stumbled across the solution: He would send to Africa his other children in Europe, who already knew the Word. Indeed the white missionaries—valiant men like Dr. Livingstone—heard the call and braved treacherous seas and jungles and disease to bring our ancestors Christianity.[13]

In reality, the "Curse of Ham" theory was used extensively to justify this type of thinking. It is a flawed interpretation, a Christian myth, and an embellished logic for explaining the origin of Black peoples. The environment for the development of this logic required a great deal of erasure of the Black kingdoms of antiquity in Nubia, Egypt, and Ethiopia.[14] These histories, belief systems, and their peoples were regarded as empty vessels for replacement. The fragile strategies also mutated and evolved as they interacted with other tools of invasion.

One particular debate was that of monogenism versus polygenism. Monogenism is the idea that all members of the human race descended from one man, Adam, while polygenism is the notion that there are multiple points of origin, thus justifying using racial differences as evidence for differentiated species. This is where the tools of religion and science experienced some conflict but ultimately used both sides of the conflict to expand anti-Blackness. In addition, White men from Europe and North America were producing ideas, beliefs, and interpretation in both of these areas, both eliminating contributions of women from the ecosystems of understanding, but also subjugating them at the same time. This will be revisited in the section on science as a tool of invasion.

If religion loses some of its grip on social construction, it also loses status, thus creating room for other unifying ideas—for example, what would come to be known as science. No longer was the assumption that it was God's command enough authority, now invaders had to expand with the imposition of science and the agreement of scholars. Here, empire, science, and wealth facilitated invention and discovery and used universities as spearheads so that White power made the task of "Western scholarship, in particular, easy enough."[15] The connection of disciplines was overlapping, like the strands of the rope in the tools of invasion, but philosophy granted science a "monopoly on truth in the marketplace of ideas, to the dismay of both artists and theologians."[16] Religion, however, did not diminish as a tool used in the colonial machinery. Misguided religious zeal tied to an appetite for conquest led to many destructive paths for colonizer and colonized alike, which also fed into notions of empire.

Empire

Of the tools considered in this chapter, empire is the broadest descriptor we use and is introduced primarily to focus on some of the most observable, confrontational, and aggressive tools of acquisition—military and legal force. As a matter of offering a basic definition, we draw from the work of historian Harari: "An empire is a political order with two important characteristics; first, to qualify for that designation you have to rule over a significant number of distinct peoples, each possessing a different cultural identity and a separate territory... Second, empires are characterized by flexible borders, and a potentially unlimited appetite."[17] Typically, military force comes first, in order to impose and maintain the acquisition. The details of the imposition reveal an initial layer of tension, in that soldiers may have been coerced in their arrival and implored to intimidate the people inhabiting the territory they are invading. Wars, enslavement, genocide, isolation, and deportation are all common mechanisms or byproducts to the initiation of empire. Legal mechanisms follow, so that the maintenance of the invasion does not have to rely on perpetual and overt military engagement.

In the review of each tool, it is critical to include a reflection on the disposition of what existed prior to invasion. This is one way of countering the idea of empty lands and vessels that needed to or came to be occupied without conflict. Of the nine theoretical dispositions outlined by Williams in *The Destruction of Black Civilization*, three are particularly relevant here:

- Blacks were among the very earliest builders of a great civilization on this planet, including the development of writing, sciences, engineering, medicine, architecture, religion, and the fine arts.
- The story of how such an advanced civilization was lost is one of the greatest and most tragic in the history of mankind and should be the main focus of research studies in African history....
- The strength and greatness of the African people can be measured by how, in the face of what at times seemed to be all the forces of hell, they fought through it all to survive and rebuild kingdoms and empires, some of which endured a thousand years.[18]

The spirit of these dispositions is often lost in the anti-Black and deficit-oriented considerations in scholarship on coloniality that examines the destruction without recognition of the achievements. Proper recognition of achievement is often limited by White and Western scholarship about continents like Africa and is controlled through mechanisms of scholarship, such as journals and universities modeled after those in Europe.[19]

An underlying root cause of the tool of empire is the notion of superiority. In order to take possession of a place, there not only has to be a deep and unyielding desire for conquest but a general assertion that an entire people's group, culture, or tribe is on the inferior side of a socially constructed dichotomy. The ability to characterize other people groups in such an inferior construction was heavily supported by religion and science. Through religious justifications or positivistic codifications, empire then generated a control of the state that had to be ruled by law and the dichotomy of what was legal or illegal. Dichotomies of empire allowed for the removal of consideration for other ways of knowing, thinking, and constructing. Legal or illegal is all that matters in the eyes of the law, and this dichotomy was enforced throughout the colonized territories of the Global South. An almost universal dominance emerged: "Hegemonic globalizations are in fact globalized localisms, the new cultural imperialism. Hegemonic globalization can be defined as the process by which a given local phenomena... succeeds in extending its reach over the globe, and by doing so develops the capacity to designate a rival social phenomenon as local."[20] The desire for dominion in the name of king and country led to the intense denial of other peoples, cultures, and knowledges. These systematic actions were essential to not only maintain a central dichotomy (i.e., superior/inferior) but also to reproduce denial through the use of other dichotomous tools such as true/false, illegal/legal, moral/amoral, civilized/barbarous, or intelligent/ignorant. In these polemicized dichotomies there is no room for dialogue or complexity, only tyranny.

The strategies of empire provided the necessary mechanisms to extract value in the form of forced labor, pillaging natural resources, creation of unequal legal treaties, displacing large portions of people, variations of apartheid, cultural destruction, and wars of various kinds. A poignant example of this is the unique and disastrous arrangement of the Congo Free State in 1885 under King Leopold II of Belgium. In an extraordinary act of rule by extension, the king claimed much of the Congo basin as his own (as opposed to an extension of Belgium). He convinced other powers in the world of the legitimacy of this arrangement by communicating a ruse of philanthropic intentions. Though he never visited the territory, he forcibly extracted ivory, rubber, and minerals by enacting violence on the residents of the land. International pressure led to the end of the scandal in 1908, but it all began as a humanitarian effort, which affirmed the dualistic notion that "modern humanity is not conceivable without modern sub-humanity."[21]

Colonialism, best reified through the enactment of laws about everything from land rights and trade regulation to socially constructed categories of race, was easily moldable according to the logics and instincts of the colonizer. For example, laws regulated social relationships like marriage between races and had to be pliable in order to continue to justify the weak principles upon which they were constructed (consider South Africa's Prohibition of Mixed Marriages Act in 1949). The "otherness" of those being colonized was not inherent or stable, but the constructions of empire needed the difference to be clearly "defined and maintained."[22] The production of colonial knowledge did not stay within colonized borders but diffused through the rapidly spreading and readily portable tool of Enlightenment era science.

Science

Science is not independent and objective research floating in an orbit detached from the other imagined orders of society. Money is required to fund research, and the acquisition of resources is often inspiration for funding research. This was the case in the invasion of Egypt in 1768 by Napoleon, whose entourage included 165 scholars. It was impossible to distinguish whether it was scientific expeditions that protected by the militaristic empire or the other way around. According to Harari, "The scientific revolution and modern imperialism were inseparable," and "The feedback loop between science, empire, and capital has arguably been history's chief engine for the past 500 years."[23]

Returning to the question of how mass cooperation is organized in human history, one common issue is that of otherness of persons in invaded lands. This constructed otherness was not innate or stable, and it had to be manufactured, legitimized, and routinely maintained. The process requires imaginary hierarchies. The consistency of a social construction does not mean it is lacking in reality (its actuality can be understood by its impacts). Harari explains that in order to maintain social imaginaries, "you always insist that the order sustaining society is an objective reality created by the great gods, or by the laws of nature... You also educate people thoroughly, from the moment they are born you constantly remind them of the principles, and of the imagined order which are incorporated into anything and everything. They are incorporated into fairytales, dramas, paintings, songs, etiquette, political propaganda, architecture, recipes, and fashions... The humanities in social sciences devote most of their energies to explaining exactly how they imagine order as woven into the tapestry of life."[24] Racial hierarchy is dependent on pseudoscience and a faith in the fixed nature of the categories. Furthermore, the categories have to include some element of contamination so as to promote disgust within the normative group. Science as portrayed by societies and universities played a critical role in the maintenance of hierarchy and difference to justify the many forms of subjugation.

An invasion of a territory with notions of superiority and metonymic dualities has disastrous effects because knowledge systems exist everywhere in the world and are manifested through language, culture, observation, experimentation, failure, and success. In the ecosystem of knowledges throughout the globe, conquest and visions of inferiority were created to eradicate epistemological difference: "I designate epistemicide, the murder of knowledge. Unequal exchanges among cultures have always implied the death of the knowledge of the subordinated culture, hence the death of the social groups that possess it. In the most extreme cases, such as that of European expansion, epistemicide was one of the conditions of genocide. The loss of epistemological confidence that currently afflicts modern science has facilitated the identification of the scope and gravity of the epistemicides perpetrated by hegemonic Eurocentric modernity."[25] Modern science has a monopoly on distinguishing between what is rendered true and false. The labels "scientific" and "nonscientific" are applications and claims to a universal validity. As previously alluded to, there is some conflict among truth claims of religion, the scientific method, and philosophy. The tragic irony in the case of the tools of invasion is that even among their conflicting epistemological dispositions, they perpetuate anti-Blackness even in disagreement. The assumption that there is no scientific knowledge in a culture (nonexistence) combined with an assumption of rigor of knowledge production produces a distinct monoculture in ways of knowing. The monoculture in turn produces a logic for social classification by naturalizing difference in categories like race and sex.[26]

The emergence of understanding race in combination with science has a volatile and contested history. There is an ongoing quest to discern when and how the social construct of race actually emerged and what the resulting impact has been.[27] Though many studies provide useful insights, the elusive moment of origin is not our highest concern. Race exists because of racism, and anti-Blackness preceded (and may outlast) any contemporary notions of racism and the construct of race.

Racism was apparent and manifest in science. The transition from religious to scientific explanations for complex questions of humans and society goes back to the conflict between monogenesis and polygenesis. The former has roots in the Christian belief that humans are an undivided species descended from Adam, the biblical figure of the first human. The monogenesis argument has as its central premise that human beings have shared humanity. Polygenesis came to undermine monogenesis in the mid-1800s with a view that there are multiple origins of the human species. Though popularized in the nineteenth century, the view had been around for two centuries as a topic of discussion in pamphlets and as scholarly societies honed the scientific Western gaze toward peoples of darker complexions. The polygenesis viewpoint separates humanity into races and makes room for a hierarchy.

Racial classifications and hierarchies emerged in multiple places with varying degrees of anti-Blackness. In 1684, the physician Francois Bernier published what would become a popular phenotypic classification that distinguished four races, promoting the notion of White Europeans as the first humans in an act of White normativity cased in science.[28] German anatomist Johann Blumenbach also published what would become a popular hierarchical classification in 1776 titled *On the Natural Variety of Man*. Though he was a monogenist, the classification system was anti-Black. Out of his five classifications for race (Caucasian, Mongolian, Malayan, Ethiopian, and American), he deemed Adam and Eve as the first humans and also Caucasian. The other races developed, according to his theory of degeneration, through inhospitable climates and living conditions that created lesser humans within his racial hierarchy. In 1863, the Anthropological Society of London was formed with the purpose of breaking away from the monogenesis-focused Ethnological Society. The new society employed strategies of phrenology and gradations of species connected to animals to explain and explore biological notions of race.[29]

The Royal Society (beginning in 1660) sent questionnaires out with world travelers and came to be a storehouse for information about skin color, behavior, and other physical observations made while people began to sail to all corners of the globe. One of the founders of the society was Robert Boyle, an Eton College graduate, natural philosopher, and monogenist. His original cadre was organized under the name "The Invisible College," and after formalizing the society, he coordinated and inspired a multifaceted system in which the reports of European travelers were used to create new queries and reports. "As natural scientists brought information about non-European people into the home to be evaluated, empiricism became the site of a knowledge-authority linked with colonial institutions."[30] The scientist/observer's view of Indigenous subjects cemented a racialized scientific approach, centering skin color as the cause (or locus) of variation between people groups. The systematic ranking of human beings according to pigmentation created an obsessive fascination with skin color.

This combination of obsession with skin color, the absence of any appreciative inquiry into Indigenous cultures and knowledges, and the commitment to difference and hierarchy was not a healthy or productive approach to research, but it was the basis for empiricism. It was combined with measuring skulls, noses, and describing hair texture to form a racialized science that produced thousands of classifications and comparisons. These metonymic and narrow approaches ignored any possibility that an ecology of knowledges might occupy a central place in the inquiry. The ecology of knowledges "challenges universal and abstract hierarchies of powers, that through them have been naturalized by history," and it recognizes the presence of knowledge before the invasion of scientific empiricism and obsession with the construction of race."[31] Using the history of science to understand this tool of invasion is an invitation to a deep reflection on Western science as a monopolistic knowledge.

Furthermore, the hierarchical dualism of sex and gender also played a role, as women were excluded from both education and science, creating more layers of oppression. As women worked to gain access to scientific and educational spaces, they began to enter a structure built around linear and dualistic logic by White European men. Going back to the Royal Society, the first women to be admitted were Kathleen Lonsdale and Marjory Stephenson in 1945—almost 300 years after its formation. Over a decade later the first person with any African descent—Emmanuel Amoroso—was admitted as a fellow to the society. Our intent is to continue to acknowledge the sovereignty of identities, peoples, cultures, the multiplicity of cognitive perspectives, and to recognize and resist the notion that oppression is always the product of a unique application of the combination of knowledges and powers. Without women's ways of knowing, Black ingenuity, and Indigenous knowledges, the ecosystem of understanding is incomplete. This history of codified knowledge through universities and its machinery of exclusion has severely limited understanding of human capacity and knowledge.

The interaction between the imperial/colonial project and scientific study created a circuit of reinforced energy fed by religious and ideological justifications, resulting in a rampant conquest mentality among White Europeans. The imperial powers supported the scientists with funding for data collection, protection, transportation, and the support to spread the scientific method around the world. As a result, "there are very few scientific disciplines that did not begin their lives as servants to imperial growth and that do not owe a large portion of their discoveries and collections, buildings, and scholarships to the generous help of army officers, navy captains, and imperial governors. This is obviously not the whole story, science was supported by other institutions, not just by empires, and the European empire grows and flourishes things to all sorts of factors other than science. Behind the meteoric rise of both science and empire there's one particularly important force, capitalism."[32] The last tool of invasion, or strand in the intertwined rope, is the leveraging of economy and the search for additional margin or capital.

Capitalism/Economy

The purpose of the scientific revolution was framed as improvement, progress, and the replacement of ignorance with empirical knowledge. It did not take long for the idea of progress in knowledge to translate into discovery, innovation, and invention that drove production and wealth. There were not only endless discoveries to make, but there was also a perpetual lust for generating economic growth. The economic system of capitalism is built on not only the belief in, but also the complete reliance on, an unremitting future growth. In the same way, the growth of science cannot be understood without capitalist economy, and capitalism cannot be understood without science.[33] A capitalist economy is the fourth strand in the powerful design of invasion. It begins with the creation of currency or money as a symbol of fungibility and exchange.

Currency represents stored and tradable value that becomes the foundation for organizing society around values. Direct bartering for goods and services preserved a more direct understanding and experience of what an item might be worth. The stored value of currency both complicated and distorted that understanding, which paved the way for economic systems and philosophies.

Preceding the emergence of capitalism, the dominant social system in Europe was feudalism. In this system, the monarch would grant sections of land to other nobles in exchange for a variety of services, goods, or protection. Knights played a role in the protective functions of the kingdom, and serfs were at the lowest end of the division of labor. Capitalism developed and was determined in form by the "social and ideological composition of a civilization that had assumed its fundamental perspectives during feudalism."[34] At the highest end of the feudal system was the monarch, whose position was established and passed down through bloodlines, creating a deterministic form of existence for everyone in the social system.

Slavery was not well known in feudal Europe, and during the transition from the Middle Ages to the early modern period, capitalism emerged along with slavery. Much of Europe was in debt (because of the notion of borrowing currency) and was looking for access to various goods that were monopolized through trade routes. In addition, precious metals became the method of payment for commercial trade, creating demand for a wide variety of materials no longer available in Europe. At the end of the fifteenth century, Spain had been involved in a multicentury battle to control the land occupied by Arabs. It became a holy war between Christianity and Islam, and Spain unified by battling with swords and crosses and a drained treasury. All of this was the backdrop for Columbus sailing across the ocean in 1492. Only three years later he invaded Haiti with cavalry, soldiers, and dogs, decimating the Native peoples and shipping five hundred of them to be enslaved in Seville.[35]

This particular moment in history demonstrates how the tools of invasion worked interdependently and set course for the next five hundred years of hegemonic globalization, anti-Blackness, and ultimately White supremacy. Spain, in conjunction with the Catholic Church, developed a demand called the Requerimiento that was read (untranslated) to Native peoples before they were physically overtaken. The last section of the statement reads:

> Y si así no lo hicieseis o en ello maliciosamente pusieseis dilación, os certifico que con la ayuda de Dios nosotros entraremos poderosamente contra vosotros, y os haremos guerra por todas las partes y maneras que pudiéramos, y os sujetaremos al yugo y obediencia de la Iglesia y de Sus Majestades, y tomaremos vuestras personas y de vuestras mujeres e hijos y los haremos esclavos, y como tales los venderemos y dispondremos de ellos como Sus Majestades mandaren, y os tomaremos vuestros bienes, y os haremos todos los males y daños que

pudiéramos, como a vasallos que no obedecen ni quieren recibir a su señor y le resisten y contradicen; y protestamos que las muertes y daños que de ello se siguiesen sea a vuestra culpa y no de Sus Majestades, ni nuestra, ni de estos caballeros que con nosotros vienen.[36]

But, if you do not do this, or maliciously make delay in it, I certify to you that, with the help of God, we shall powerfully enter into your country, and shall make war against you in all ways and manners that we can, and shall subject you to the yoke and obedience of the Church and of their Highnesses; we shall take you and your wives and your children, and shall make slaves of them, and as such shall sell and dispose of them as their Highnesses may command; and we shall take away your goods, and shall do all the mischief and damage that we can, as to vassals who do not obey, and refuse to receive their lord, and resist and contradict him; and we protest that the deaths and losses which shall accrue from this are your fault, and not that of their Highnesses, or ours, nor of these cavaliers who come with us.

Conflict, necessity, claims to a higher power, and belief in infinite growth due to constructions of superiority came together in a powerful way.

Cedric Robinson outlines four important moments to discern under the umbrella of European racialism. The first is the racial organization of European society from its formation through the feudal society focus on bloodlines. The second is the Islamic domination of Mediterranean civilization (especially Spain) and the depression of European social life through the Dark Ages. The third is the incorporation of African and Asian peoples into the world that emerged from the systems of feudalism and merchant capitalism. The fourth is the widespread colonialism involving slavery and the foundations for industrial labor.[37] Robinson emphasizes that many studies of racism look at points of first contact with African peoples and then colonialism but ignore feudalism and Islamic domination. He also adds that history should not "revolve around European peoples or . . . originate from Europe as in the center."[38]

The pursuit of never-ending economic growth fueled a hostile entry into worlds that were considered empty and inferior. Financial fascism is a vicious control of social systems with a market mentality: "The flows of capital are the result of the decisions of individual or institutional investors spread out all over the world, and having nothing in common except the desire to maximize their assets."[39] Connecting to the appetite for conquest, turning land, resources, and people into fungible, currency-based market items, is a fundamental core of the ongoing settler colonial mentality that drives human and social relationships. Structures and motives are increasingly organized around tradable value and the production of building capital to fuel the myth of an ever-expanding opportunity to accumulate.

The oppressive structures built within this disposition are exposed by descriptions of racial capitalism. The roots of the tools of invasion are still alive and thriving. By way of brief example, international economic development is built on the notion that some societies are in poverty and others that are wealthy have the means and conditions to "help" develop the rest. The tyranny of this kind of expertise[40] is exposed by the profound truth that the best evidence that international development does not work is all of human history—none of the world's wealthiest countries got that way because of a World Bank or International Monetary Fund loan. Many of them achieved their status of wealth through economic capitalism and other tools of invasion. Only through the existence of an entity as rich can something else be poor. Rich and poor are not essentialized identities; they describe a relationship to the whole that is organized by capitalism.

Conclusions on the Crux of the Matter

Exploration, acquisition, and theft of land were different approaches to expansion, compared to the migration patterns of the hunters, gatherers, and foragers who slowly made their way around the Earth in previous centuries of human expansion. The way European countries were willing to set out into uncharted waters with a determination and a desire to discover and acquire territories was both innovative and disturbing. In a few centuries (beginning in the sixteenth and increasing with intensity over time), several European powers had conquered key parts of the globe and claimed it for the homeland. Other superpowers of exploration in the world during this time of conquest (e.g., China and India) also engaged in expanding their empires. However, the European powers set forth with a distinct mission to simultaneously discover, claim, conquer, and tame the corners of Earth.

Desire binds the tools together and provides some distinction from the technological prowess and empires in other places around the world. In *Open Veins of Latin America*, Eduardo Galeano outlines five hundred years of the pillaging of a continent for its resources. From precious metals to people, sugar, oil, and so on, the historical structure of invasion shaped the contemporary structure of plunder, which makes understanding these tools and their relationship to knowledge production and universities an essential task for this study. In an effort to examine our own dispositions in relationship to anti-Blackness and its structure within universities, we begin each case study with an in-depth examination and appreciation of what preceded invasion and what persists in spite of invasion. As a matter of understanding the application of the tools, we first examine the development and distinction of the White homeland and the White diaspora in the next chapter.

2

Homeland, Diaspora, and Traveling Whiteness

> Afrikaans is the language that connects Western Europe and Africa ... It forms a bridge between the large, shining West and the magical Africa ... And what great things may come from their union—that is maybe what lies ahead for Afrikaans to discover. But what we must never forget, is that this change of country and landscape sharpened, kneaded and knitted this newly-becoming language ... And so Afrikaans became able to speak out from this new land ...
> —Quote from the Afrikaans Language Museum in Paarl, South Africa (translated)

Homelands and diasporas are different sides of the same concept. White European citizens may have loved their countries and cultures, but for various economic, military, religious, or political reasons they either sought or served expansion elsewhere through settler travels and "discovery" of lands already inhabited by other peoples. Sometimes homesick and displaced, they longed to recreate some semblance of their homeland wherever they relocated, and they claimed newly conquered land in the name of God, king, and country as they reestablished White European values, norms, and practices in their new worlds. These endeavors often led to forced religious conversions, forced enslavement, land theft, and systemic reeducation policies and practices inflicted upon Native and Indigenous peoples.

Our goal in this chapter is to track the ways in which White European cultural practices traveled from the homeland but rematerialized in an altered state in new lands. What emerged in other colonized and stolen lands was a reified and mutated diasporic version of White dominance inflicted upon already existing societies and cultures. A traveling Whiteness originating in the homeland center dispersed to the diasporic periphery and persisted in dominance with a paradoxical composition in the so-called "new worlds." In this chapter we track the ways in which ideas and power shifted across Western Europe to a North American continuum, as both places powerfully represented an ideological homeland. As conquests drifted throughout the Global South, the distant communities created a White diaspora that in many ways replicated the racist ideologies of the homeland in new locations around the globe.

We define the White homeland as an ideological ethnostate whereby White people are coercively positioned at the top of the hierarchical and socially constructed superstructure by way of an ill-conceived notion of divine birthright. This notion of a hierarchical birthright has evolved through various religious and pseudoscientific dispositions used to justify White purity, providence, and paternal duty. The ideological homeland, then, became the framework in striving for permanent White global supremacy and dominance. One of the key bases of the White homeland was the development of racial classifications to demarcate Whiteness above all others.

Diasporas are generally about peoples dispossessed and exiled from their homeland (e.g., the Black, Korean, or Jewish diaspora). Movements of people are rooted in a traditional understanding of the diaspora saga as the involuntary nature of displacement and loss. This moves beyond the loss of a homeland to include the loss or alteration of heritage language, artifacts, and culture. The White homeland of Europe sent out voluntary invaders with promises of riches and heroism. In the voluntary yet unintentional diasporas, the heritage, language, and ideology was not lost but rather adapted for different regions to maintain dominance. The invaders took the seeds of Whiteness and planted them in distant soil, and when they returned to the homeland they were treated more like some version of a foreigner as a result of their altered habits, speech patterns, and perspectives. The evolution in their Whiteness was not because of the seeds but because of the soil where they settled.

The White European diasporic phenomenon ultimately continued to the decimation of Indigenous homelands and, in turn, forced a diaspora for Indigenous peoples. The White search for conquest generated Native captivity and forced removals. These White diasporas ultimately generated other diasporas around the world through displacement. There is a distinct homeland/diaspora paradox: the pursuit of feeling something familiar from a homeland while simultaneously being rejected by it. Layers of rejection cement a new and distant identity that fits neither at home nor in the new settlement, thus creating a diaspora.

Even voluntary decisions can be rooted in having no other choice but to seek refuge elsewhere. Poor working-class White Europeans might have felt compelled to make certain voluntary choices due to economic inequality, or else were in search of new opportunities like property ownership. Some were understandably driven into involuntary migration as a result of imprisonment and expeditions to penal colonies, as was the case in Australia. There are White diasporic myths and grand narratives that have transcended time and guided the ideology and practices for White European settlers around the world. Whiteness and an ideology of suffering can be rooted in the stories of those who colonized, settled, and seized other lands.

Expansion

Some of the original global colonizers and invaders hailed from nations such as France, Belgium, Spain, Portugal, Great Britain, and The Netherlands. Ideological power shifted to the United States through a period of immigration and the so-called pursuit of "enlightenment." The sources of knowledge were symbiotic, but the United States was using all the tools of invasion to justify the destruction of Indigenous peoples and the enslavement of Africans forced into the "American colonies." Colonization is an interconnected history of the removal of the Indigenous from their lands in the Americas, Oceania, and Africa. Religious justifications for dominance were used and consequently debated in the earliest American colonies to explore the difference among races. The pursuit of phrenology was active in both Europe and the United States, but the robustness of its application and the expanse of science and capitalism founded upon racist principles produced a new global superpower in the United States—founded on principles used to justify racist practices while claiming liberty and justice for all. As universities expanded in the United States, the presence of enslaved Africans was prominent, as was the development of racist science (e.g., eugenics) and economics (e.g., racial capitalism).[1] In this way, the perceptions of race in connection with university-sponsored knowledge production contributed to the concept of the homeland and diaspora.

A major shift in European society was a push away from the feudal medieval social system in the 1500s. Feudalism was characterized by a monarch providing lands to a noble class who in exchange provided military service. Additionally, the lowest class of serfs worked the lands of the nobility in exchange for military protection. The major decline in feudalism came with the Crusades to reclaim holy lands that were occupied by Muslims. In addition, new trade routes opened up, beginning the reach of kingdoms beyond their borders. Commodities such as spices from India, silk and silver from China, and precious metals like gold and silver from Africa became markers of status, wealth, and personal glory.

As the thirst for wealth exploded, the appetite for conquest became an insignia in the emerging capitalist regime. The insatiable desire for economic growth led to expeditions with royal investments in conquest, each one in search of more efficient trading routes and eventually "new" lands to generate wealth. The Spanish, Portuguese, British, French, and Dutch undertook campaigns of maritime expeditions with the explicit aims of claiming land, searching for untapped natural resources, and scientific discovery. Merchants such as Christopher Columbus, Amerigo Vespucci, and Ferdinand Magellan have been canonized into a historical lexicon as benevolent explorers, conveniently erasing the clear and apparent mission directive to pillage, plunder, and commence genocide. The explicit commission sought the expansion of the kingdom, emphasizing the acquiring of land for the primary purpose of the forcible extraction of wealth. These were some of the earliest colonizing departures from the homeland.

Knowledge Production for a White Homeland

Through the late fifteenth, sixteenth, and early seventeenth centuries, Christianity became fractured through the Reformation (sixteenth century), which politically challenged the Roman Catholic power structure and created subsections of protestant denominations. This ideological splintering gave an opening to science and pseudoscience, which filled the chasm with ideas of objectivity, truth, and discovery. As noted in chapter 1 on the tools of invasion, science and religion were harmonious for the purposes of racial dominance and subordination in establishing a White homeland.

Similar to the religious justifications for the subordination of the Global South, European scientists played an equally destructive role in this process. This tension is succinctly captured by physicist Chanda Prescod-Weinstein: "Indeed, it was a supposedly enlightened Europe that enshrined the animus toward darker-skinned people in its colonial satellites as a tool to help maintain a unidirectional flow of resources, from the colonies to the heart of empire. Rather than skeptically considering the substance of these colonial sensibilities, scientists largely sought to substantiate them through a search for their scientific foundations. Science thus became a process in which bias was consecrated by scientists. Racism was axiomatic, rather than a belief requiring skeptical investigation."[2] A prominent example of this racist notion of science is found in Jean Riolan II, a French anatomist who was the "spiritual head of Paris Medical School."[3] Riolan was described as a man of national pride, who had strong convictions about the cultural mission of France. In 1626, Riolan claimed to have dissected more than one hundred bodies, one of which was an Ethiopian male cadaver. He demonstrated his keen interest in African skin by trying to find a cause for what we would now understand as the function of melanin. The meticulous obsession is demonstrated in figure 8.

The frenetic interest in African physiology—stemming from both religious and scientific inquiry—was, of course, inherently racist. These White scientists were not desecrating White bodies to uncover what makes European skin white. This othering of Black bodies was firmly rooted in anti-Blackness. Andrew Curran explains in *The Anatomy of Blackness* that "anatomists were seen as able to pronounce on what was most appropriate to humankind's 'way of life' and the fulfillment of its needs."[4] Through the status and prestige of a university professorship, anatomists used physiology and anatomy to justify White dominance and the predestination of, in this case, Black bodies towards subjugation.

The systematizing of racial categories and groups was an attempt to maintain European power and dominance. Patrick Wolfe writes in *Traces of History: Elementary Structures of Race*, "Subjugated populations are racialized in distinct but complementary ways that together sustain the overall dominance of European colonisers."[5] Race was introduced by Europeans as a way to separate and justify the exploitation and annihilation of those perceived to be different than the White Europeans. Religious and pseudoscientific justifications were all in line with notions of White European superiority and moral authority. Charles R. Mills concisely critiques this notion of race in his book *The Racial Contract* by stating:

> The economic dimension of the Racial Contract is the most salient, foreground rather than background, since the Racial Contract is calculatedly aimed at economic exploitation. The whole point of establishing a moral hierarchy and juridically partitioning the polity according to race is to secure and legitimate the privileging of those individuals designated as white/persons and the exploitation of those individuals designated as nonwhite/subpersons. There are other benefits accruing from the Racial Contract—far greater political influence, cultural hegemony, the psychic payoff that comes from knowing one is a member of the Herrenvolk (what W. E. B. Du Bois once called "the wages of whiteness")—but the bottom line is material advantage. Globally, the Racial Contract creates Europe as the continent that dominates the world; locally, within Europe and the other continents, it designates Europeans as the privileged race.[6]

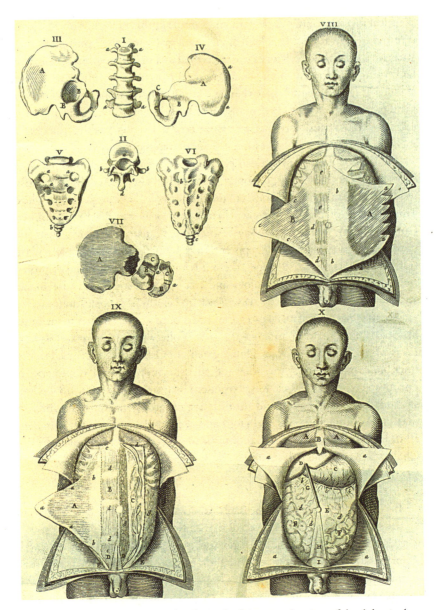

FIGURE 8 Jean Riolan II, *A Manual in the Study of Anatomy*, drawings of the abdominal muscles, lumbar vertebrae, pelvic bones, and sacrum of an Ethiopian man. The Thomas Fisher Rare Book Library, University of Toronto.

This notion of the privileged race was foundational to the creation of the White homeland, which was a conduit of what David Theo Goldberg refers to as the racial state. Goldberg writes, "Racial states employ physical force, violence, coercion, manipulation, deceit, cajoling, incentives, law(s), taxes, penalties, surveillance, military force, repressive apparatuses, ideological mechanisms and media—in short, all the means at a state's disposal—ultimately to the ends of racial rule."[7] The racial codification that Goldberg describes creates a White homeland that is not simply a geographical region measured in square kilometers, but an ideological terrain without borders. This idea of a borderless culture ultimately became the White diaspora.

Historian Craig Steven Wilder argued that the very nature of science was redeveloped and repackaged to justify and ensure the ongoing enslavement of Black Africans. He writes:

> The academy refined and legitimated the social ideas that supported territorial expansion, a process that transformed the people of the new nation from revolutionaries to imperialists. It advanced the project through which the United States extended its borders across the North American mainland. Jefferson had access to researchers who were a recent addition to American society. Colonial students had been crowding the medical and science programs of Europe for two generations, carrying the political and social beliefs and desires of their communities to the intellectual centers of the Atlantic World. Students from North America crafted a science that justified expansionism and slavery—a science that generated broad claims to expertise over colored people and thrived upon unlimited access to nonwhite bodies. They did not abandon the search for truth; they redefined truth.[8]

His last statement bears repeating: scholars did not abandon the search for truth, but redefined it. Scientists directed knowledge production to fit their economic, theological, and White dominant needs.

Indigenous Homelands Prior to Invasion

For generations before the colonizers arrived, the Indigenous of these lands developed thriving and sustainable civilizations. In present day North and South America, Oceania, and Southern Africa, the areas that serve as the focus of our inquiry, all had cultures that flourished independently of European interference and disruption. Shifting our lens from the perspective of the explorers to the civilizations that existed for centuries prior to their arrival is important in understanding how and why the White homelands were created.

Generations of Indigenous tribes lived in what is now called North America, pursuing a communal focus on the land as a sacred place that gives sustenance to the living world, including the flora, fauna, fowl, and big-game mammals. For thousands of years, the Indigenous nations emphasized harmony with nature revolving around a core idea of only taking what you need from the land. Foraging and hunting for food was a sustainable way of life for the Indigenous. A key hallmark of Indigenous collective cultures was the "Seventh Generation" approach that took into consideration the decisions they made in the present and how they might affect their people several generations from that time point.[9] A famous Indigenous saying, which brings this point to life, is, "When the last tree is cut down, the last fish eaten, and the last stream poisoned, you will realize that you cannot eat money."[10] At the core is a notion of responsibility and sustainability. Indigenous knowledge and spirituality focused on maintaining balance with the ecosystem with a strong emphasis on the interconnection of all life. The worldview of the Indigenous tribes of the Seminole, Catawba, Powhatan, Susquehannock, Shawnee, Massachuset, Sioux, Iroquois, Apache, Choctaw, Navajo, and Cherokee among others was in stark contrast to that of the European invaders.

The Indigenous in South America (Tupinambá, Tapuia, Arawak, Carib, Aimoré, Gaurani, and Ge) were hunters, gatherers, fishers, and farmers. They cultivated a wide variety of crops, unlike monoagriculture in Europe. They developed preservation techniques to store harvests underground, which allowed civilization to flourish. The richness of the lands with a canopy of trees for miles on end, rivers flowing, and an abundance of wildlife like flocks of colorful toucans created a beautiful tapestry of life in precolonial Brazil. The peoples of these lands spoke hundreds of distinct languages and dialects. Of interest to invaders were Brazil's vast deposits of diamonds, jade, copper, and many other minerals.

The creation story for the Māori is laid out in three major cycles: the sky, the earth, and broadly the relationship and benefits of nature to humankind. The personification of nature in the Māori narrative is a foundational indicator of the holistic worldview. Humans were created as "belonging to the land: as tangata whenua, people of the land."[11] In this way, they are not above the rest of nature but interdependent and within nature. This origin dictates a meaningful and ongoing relationship characterized by reverence. For Polynesians living in Samoa and Tonga in the millenniums preceding their arrival in Aotearoa, integration with the natural surroundings produced an incredible ability to navigate the vast ocean using the stars while sailing in double-hulled canoes made from trees. The ability to traverse thousands of miles of ocean preceded Columbus by seven centuries. The establishment of language, tribes, family units, integration with nature, hunting, navigating, and the maintenance of society through deep belief systems is an incredible history of knowledge production and diffusion that was threatened by colonization, but which persists throughout Oceania today.

For over five thousand years, Black civilizations prospered on the continent of Africa. In regions in present day Egypt, Mali, Ethiopia, Ghana, Sudan, Niger, and Nigeria (to name a few), these advanced cultures mastered geometry, writing, geography, astronomy, nautical travel, farming, and mining. Vast empires were established, like the reign of Mansa Musa in Islamic Mali during the early 1300s. Mansa Musa's hajj (pilgrimage to Mecca) through Cairo was notable because the monarch displayed such generosity in showering hosts with gifts of gold. He had roughly three hundred pounds of gold, which is equivalent to $6.7 million (in 2021 USD). He returned to Mali without any of the gold remaining; he had given it all away during his hajj.[12] It was reported that "as a result of the extravagance of the Sudanese and the lavish generosity of their monarch, so much gold was suddenly put into circulation in Egypt that its market value fell sharply and had not recovered" for over ten years.[13] Vast trade routes were established to Northern Africa in order to trade with Asians and Europeans. Africa is the most natural-resource-rich continent on the planet with enormous deposits of diamonds, gold, and an abundance of minerals. White dominant narratives characterized the civilizations of Africa as a monolith with insistence that they needed saving because "Africans" lived a subhuman life prior to the Western Europeans' arrival. However, the lesser-known story of Mansa Musa shatters any misconception about all Africans living a destitute existence prior to the Western European invasion of African societies.

Carrying the flag of the homeland, White Europeans invaded and stole the lands of centuries-old societies. However, the justification for this violent genocide and subordination was in consistent need of maintenance to supersede the clear and obvious atrocities against humanity that ensued for the next five hundred years. The settler process was more than the seizing of land. It was also the domination of the mind, body, and spirit of the Indigenous and enslaved Africans—and it was a process of being away from the homeland while trying to establish authority and control in places where Whites felt ostracized. In some cases, being in the position of an underdog made the White colonizers more tenacious about supremacy than they were in the context of home (for example, the Afrikaners in South Africa). Some of the concepts used to establish a settlement in a distant land mirror the tools of invasion.

Characteristics of the White Diaspora

Imagine the first points of contact and the collision of cultures in each of these geographies. The settler reactions are recorded at length in their own journals and reports, in which they use the lenses and frameworks developed in Europe to label everything that is not European as either "savage" or "barbarous."[14] These supremacist descriptors were then used as scientific categories. "Savage" described people who lived off of the land, even worshipped it, and had no perceived social organization. "Barbarous" were those who had loose autocratic organization, engaged in some subsistence farming, and worshipped many gods. The final of the three stages is that of "civilization," which was characterized by democratic organization, productivity, manners, and monotheism. As a result, the effort to use White logic to establish White homeland values and practices in new places as new arrivals started immediately. Similar to their use of tools of invasion, they were looking to establish comforts and reminders of home: churches, commerce, education, and governance—in other words, civilization.

Religion

People who were perceived as worshiping the land or who had many gods were categorized with descriptions like "primitive" or "backwards." Churches committed to one God had to be established, not only to mirror the more "advanced" way of European civilization but as a manner of recreating home. For example, consider the Dutch merchants moving to South Africa's Cape Town (originally known as Table Bay), which was an outpost established by the Dutch United East India Company. This refueling and refreshment port in the mid-1600s eventually became an opportunity for some of the executives of the company to settle down permanently in retirement as a reward for many years of service. As they established their new home, the seeds of their religious convictions had to be planted in new soil. The Dutch Reformed Church, now on a different continent, had to be hybridized in order to adapt their beliefs and responses to the people already inhabiting the land. Their religious beliefs contributed to the earliest laws about anti-miscegenation because of the religious conviction that White and Black people could not marry.

Commerce

Goods and services needed to be created to provide the domestic comforts of home. The foundation of the White homeland is the inherent unsustainable economic growth that is needed to generate wealth. White men left their homeland for the promise of producing wealth for themselves and their future lineage, or to gain notoriety and stature as a "great man." Often funded and/or chartered by royals and nobility, the "explorers" set sail with the express aim of enriching their respective Western European nations. Unlike the sustainability of Indigenous ways of life, this quest for wealth is unsustainable and has led to the demise of many empires when further conquest and exploitation ran rampant.[15] Colonization was established as the system to spread world capitalism and was strongly rooted in social, racial, and political ideology. While initially vying for world domination as separate entities, the individual nations of the White homeland were united under a common European identity: "Internal national rivalries continued, of course, but this common identity based on the transcontinental exploitation of the non-European world would in many cases be politically crucial, generating a sense of Europe as a cosmopolitan entity engaged in a common enterprise, underwritten by race."[16] In essence, while early competition for distant lands put European nations at odds with each other, a grander picture emerged with the creation of a coalescent White identity related to the aim of domination of the Global South. Rooted in both racism and nationalism, world capitalism emerged as the dominant political and economic ideology.[17]

Governance

Laws in a European fashion were established in order to govern the "unrefined" ways of the inhabitants in the newly settled locations. Indigenous peoples and societies had an interdependent relationship with the land. The White logic and empires that moved into these spaces used paper to define relationships between land and people. Paper signified ownership, citizenship, property, and legality. All of these concepts were deemed marks of civilization. As a result, the process of trying to make a new place feel like home also coincided with what was depicted as "progress" for civilization. Regulations, laws, and governance were part of the logic systems, and the longer they persisted, the more they gained the perception of permanence and legitimacy. Within a matter of decades, the governance mentality of the White homeland became firmly established in the White diaspora. This led to a variety of policies that enabled, for example, apartheid in South Africa and the "White Australia" policy in that country. Treaties in many places were used to disadvantage Indigenous peoples, and property claims redistributed wealth and rights for the foreseeable future. Many of these details are covered further in the case study chapters, 4, 5, and 6.

Science and Education

There was a great deal of variety in terms of the people aboard the ships that landed in the soon-to-be White diasporas around the world. Those that landed in Botany Bay in Australia mainly carried prisoners. In South Africa, the earliest arrivals were merchants setting up trade routes. Members of the military often joined to offer protection, and scientists voyaged to collect data and take notes to publish in scientific proceedings in Europe. No matter the levels of education, there was agreement about the nature of education. It was formal, Eurocentric, and linear. There were principles of arithmetic, literature, philosophy, and religion that comprised the canon of thought and belief for the White mind and social structure. Over time, schools had to be established to educate not only the children in the White diaspora but also those Indigenous children in the surrounding areas. Attempts to draw Indigenous peoples into White educational systems were often just as supremacist as overt attempts to exclude them. Once the primary and secondary schools were established, they needed to create centers of knowledge production for measuring and making claims on absolute truth. The colleges and universities that were established were headed by people educated in Europe and North America, and their curriculums and even physical architecture mimicked the White homeland as well.

White-on-White Competition

Given the way that White supremacist ideology manifested itself, and the military power and violence that was required to maintain it, the actual location of foreign lands did not matter for the task of recreating home. However, the nationalistic rivalries could disrupt some of the resettlement in the absence of a unified White vision. The Dutch and British and the Spanish and Portuguese alike were rivals in some ways—but then, they all had similar agendas. They shared a common goal of expansion and conquest, and the race to rule the world for king/queen and country drove this era of colonialism and invasion. Inevitably, they would unify in pursuit of a common cause. In South Africa, for example, the British were there along with the Dutch; but eventually they united around the racial classification of White in order to subdue Black South Africans through apartheid. In similar ways, the Portuguese in Brazil were in competition with the Dutch, which led to various conflicts with one another. In the midst of the rivalries, cultural differences, and nuances between colonizing nations, there was the consistently terrible treatment of Indigenous people. The appetite for conquest included a need for a racial hierarchy, and ultimately became a conduit for competing forces within Europe to unite under the banner of racial purity and supremacy.

The White diaspora drove South Africans to become some of the most tenacious White people in the world with regard to the pursuit of White domination. The diaspora concept helps to explain Afrikaners, and it helps us understand their behavior as they embraced ownership of their new South African homeland. Even the move to Australia with the penal colonies seemed more like an opportunity for advancement for working-class convicts than like a punishment, even if they were not granted the option of leaving.

Traveling Whiteness included a change in the definitions of knowledge and intelligence. We argue that racial pseudoscience started in Europe, and that the concept then traveled with colonizers who established research and scholarship rooted in faulty ethnographic hermeneutics and eugenics. As Maori scholar Linda Tuhiwai Smith explained, research is "inextricably linked to European imperialism and colonialism. The word itself is probably one of the dirtiest words in the Indigenous world vocabulary. It is implicated in the worst excesses of colonialism, with the ways in which knowledge about

Indigenous peoples was collected, classified, and then represented back to the west."[18]

Scholars on Indigenous methodology Marie Battiste and James Youngblood Henderson offer some poignant reflection on the impact of colonialism in modern contexts.[19] They first argue that a dominant group's culture, knowledge, experiences, and language inevitably become the universal norm. They then assert that the carriers of dominance (discussed in detail in the next chapter), such as university professors, demand conformity and assimilation to these standards. Indeed, leaders in the academic and broader society have significant influence on the institutional structures, content, process, and language used by that society and are constantly reinforcing the minimalization of Indigenous knowledge.

Eurocentric ideologies have led to a misguided belief in the superiority of Western European ways of knowing over all non-European, Indigenous, and non-White people groups, cultures, and languages. This is caused by a dangerous combination of ignorance and hubris, and it is exacerbated by a hunger for dominance. Written and spoken English as the lingua franca in many universities across the nations reveals an unspoken rule that the language of dominant societies has become the accepted standard for all scholars engaged in international academic research communities. Indeed, for many institutions of higher learning, the ability to instruct and read in English has been determined to define competitive advantage on a global stage. The hegemony of language is also connected to knowledge as a consequence of colonialism. Scholars conducting research on indigeneity, such as Beverley Bailey[20] and Gregory Cajete,[21] argue that colonialism irrevocably impacted ways of knowing and radically yet negatively transformed existing Native and Indigenous education systems.

We argue that a hegemony of culture, language, art, and many other ways of knowing has been a critical tool of invasion within the academy and broader society, ever since the establishment of White European tertiary education systems outside of Europe. Battiste and Youngblood Henderson argue that the introduction of White Western knowledge systems simultaneously meant the beginning of the end of Native and Indigenous forms of knowledge production and research methods. Colonizing White European educators introduced human disciplines such as sociology and anthropology while rejecting traditional Native values, norms, customs, and ideologies.

Creating the Global Definition of White

Rich landowners or those who came from a royal lineage sought to expand their reach. If they were a poor, destitute White person, or a prisoner, then they sought to improve their lot with opportunities beyond their current station. That might have included seeking opportunities to leave the home country in pursuit of something better: adventure, land ownership, freedom, or a new start.

The historical development of the definition of White related to a larger racial classification and produced another type of traveling Whiteness. This dominant racial category changed its definition and developed legal maneuvers for person to change their racial status, making this change paradoxically achievable but hard to attain, as evidenced in South Africa and Brazil. A display in the Apartheid Museum in Johannesburg, South Africa, offers information about the number of people who changed their racial classification in 1985. According to *The Star* newspaper, the minister of home affairs disclosed that 702 colored people became White, 19 Whites became colored, one Indian became White, three Chinese became White, and 249 Black people became colored, but ultimately no Whites became Black and no Blacks became White. Conversely, there is another problem of not clearly addressing race, leading to challenges stemming from under-identification and the lack of an ability to disaggregate identities. In Australia, the broad and impractical label of "culturally and linguistically diverse" (CALD) is used without refinement. Someone from France may be CALD and therefore lumped with someone of Indian descent.

The belief in superiority and desire for dominance was memorialized in sculptured monuments of White heroes. Some of these have been contested, protested, and even brought down in recent years (e.g., Cecil Rhodes in South Africa in 2015 and the attempt on William Wentworth in Australia in 2019). The journey from White homelands (Europe/North America) to White diaspora (Australia, South Africa, Brazil) has clashed with a developing modern consciousness regarding race, equity, and inclusion. The White attempt to cling to dominance has further produced what we refer to as homeland insecurities—an ideology and desire to protect and close borders to "immigrants" and other undesirable people groups while simultaneously expanding Whiteness even further through development, Christian missions, and military defense.

In her book *The Colonial Fantasy*, Sara Maddison writes that "settler colonial studies is a relatively new field of academic scholarship. If we are to imagine a radically different set of relations between Indigenous peoples and settlers in Australia, then we must also bring new conceptual tools to this task."[22] We agree that new conceptual tools are needed to understand and convey the ideas rooted in colonial ideology. Maddison goes on to argue for a need to make explicit that which has long been implicit, to make the previously invisible but ubiquitous settler colonial ideology much more visible to all.[23] Indeed, we set as our goal to excavate the White logic systems that drove White settlers toward diaspora and extended travel.

White homelands and White diasporas are what undergird our understanding of how empire is built and sustained. These concepts of White homeland and diasporas are what carried the imperial notions from Europe and then later the United States and North America. They established various forms of cultural Whiteness wherever Europeans traveled, with some culturally nuanced differences between the ways that the British versus the Dutch conquered lands and people in South Africa and their treatment of Black South Africans versus Maori and other Aboriginal peoples in Oceania. Many White European colonizers had the same shared goals of empire-building in mind. The British and the Dutch were at war with each other and in competition, and their spoils of victory were rooted in the Native resources, the people, and the glory for king and country. In *The History of the World and Seven Cheap Things*, authors Raj Patel and Jason Moore offer a profound but simple understanding of the desire for dominion in the form of all things cheap—cheap nature, cheap money, cheap work, cheap care, cheap food, cheap energy, and cheap lives.[24] They argue that the desire for low overhead in the ownership of resources is the antecedent to capitalism, globalization, and ultimately domination.

As South African scholar Saul Dubow explains, a typical working-class Afrikaner was considered inferior by other White Europeans because he or she could not speak English well. At the same time, Afrikaners were concerned about economic competition against the many Black African tribes, in what was known as *swart gevaar*, or black peril. Christian nationalist Afrikaners very effectively played off of the fears and the perceived dangers of Black domination. They also feared miscegenation, or *bloedvermmenging*, and believed that colored and mixed-race Africans represented the defilement of the root White Afrikaner race. A combination of White pride, Afrikaner pride, and anti-Blackness drove their hatred of Black Native Africans and ultimately led to apartheid in South Africa.[25]

As farmers and low-income workers, White Afrikaners were also worried about losing jobs to Black South Africans. They grew to despise the *kaffirbowtie*, or "friends of the native." Theological interpretations based mostly on the Dutch Reformed Church and its missionaries led to a woefully deficient biblical understanding of apartheid and separation based on race. This miscarried theological understanding also influenced their own self-aggrandizing interpretation that Afrikaners were God's chosen people (in contrast to Black South Africans). The Voortrekker movement known as the Great Trek was eventually re-envisioned as a sign of the suffering and persecution of Afrikaners who made the legendary trek inland.

Afrikaner scholars and theologians alike were influenced by philosophers like Abraham Kuyper, whose Neo-Calvinist theological convictions led the Dutch Reformed Church to embrace and perpetuate anti-Blackness and ultimately apartheid. According to Indigenous scholar Jo-Anne Q'um Q'um Xiiem Archibald,[26] a critical tool of colonization was research, of which Indigenous story-taking and story-making was a vital part. Colonial Western research of the traditional stories of Indigenous peoples was manipulated to devalue and destroy Indigenous knowledge, people, and practices.

Homelands and Diasporas Reconsidered: The Turn

Whether by exploration, escape, imprisonment, or invasion, what were the results of White Western European colonials leaving their White homelands and seeking new territories for those people groups who already resided in these spaces? Native and Indigenous homelands were turned upside down, ultimately leading to both voluntary and involuntary diasporas across the globe. The history of displaced people groups is a common theme in modern history texts. The disruption of Native homelands began with diseases brought by European settlers that decimated Native people, and continued with the forced labor and enslavement of people, their displacement from their homes, the theft of their property and people, forced demarcations of land, and the creation of foreign laws. It extended to other spheres of the society as well, from forced religious conversions to the destruction of Indigenous knowledge and the recreation of educational systems, and even to clothing and fashion as a method of enlightening and civilizing the First Nations who were considered uneducated, ruthless, and godless heathens.

The additional and unforeseen fruit resulting from this invasive root was the displacement of Black, Brown, and Indigenous people, who fled seeking refuge elsewhere. Some, bound by indentured servitude, were obliged to travel back to White homelands with their new masters; those who were enslaved were then sold and disbursed to the ends of the Earth like chattel. These painful and more commonly recognized Indigenous diasporic journeys are in fact rooted in the White diaspora that preceded them. The connection between homelands and diasporas created mutually exclusive directions for the colonial settlers and the original peoples of the lands where they settled. Ultimately for White settlements, the tenacity that emerged from a diasporic disposition shaped the character of their conquests.

3

The University as Colonizer and Carrier of White Dominance

> Education as the exercise of domination
> stimulates the credulity of students, with
> the ideological intent (often not perceived
> by educators) of indoctrinating them to
> adapt to the world of oppression.[1]
> —Freire

In the Southern Hemisphere, Australia, New Zealand, South Africa, and South America (especially Brazil and Argentina) have the greatest concentrations of White people. With historical knowledge of how this took place over time, and with evidence of their unique White diasporic identities, this chapter explores the role universities play in knowledge and empire production/maintenance. From a historical exploration, we include information on knowledge production from the White homeland that created a line of diffusion through universities and societies that spread into established territories of the White diaspora.

Though the racial category of White is identified and tested differently in distinctive regions, figure 9 is a map indicating the places most populated with White people in 2018. These concentrations of race in our contemporary setting still map directly to the invasions of the Global South. The fruits of Whiteness that we experience today come from seeds that were distributed and planted hundreds of years ago. Universities played a role in that cultivation, and to

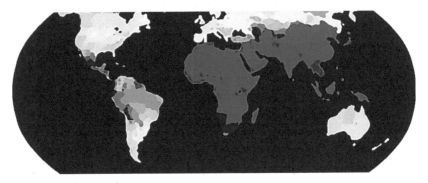

FIGURE 9 Demographic heat map showing the location of the greatest prevalence of White people in 2018. (Image created by author.)

fully understand higher education, these institutions must be situated in their colonizing context as carriers of White dominance.

The introduction of homeland educational habits and values to the lands of the diaspora created an immediate disconnect and at times violent interactions between Indigenous peoples and their colonizers. In the United States, for example, Indian boarding schools were established with the explicit goal of assimilation. In Captain Richard H. Pratt's address on Indian education in 1892, he communicated many alarming ideas and strategies, including: "Transfer the savage-born infant to the surroundings of civilization, and he will grow to possess a civilized language and habit. These results have been established over and over again beyond all question." In a direct advocation of epistemicide, he conveyed the idea that you could kill the Indian and save the man.[2] These types of schools did not save Indigenous people from anything. There were instances of kidnapping, forced labor, abuse, the spread of disease, and endangerment from children trying to escape. Curriculums and codification of knowledge historically and intentionally excluded the first knowledges of the peoples from whom the land was stolen. The land-knowledge suppression during the invasions constituted an epistemicide.[3] Indigenous and First Nations people, their ways of knowing, their traditions, and their culture were under assault either directly by force or indirectly by contact. The residue of those moments of first contact is present in a variety of contemporary manifestations, including race categories, affirmative action, pedagogy for remediation, curriculum, architecture, and the alma mater for faculty members and administrators. The early settlers were carriers of disease and ideology, both of which were sown deeply into the soils of the new White diasporas.

The South represents not only a geographic region but also a collection of epistemologies. Epistemologies of the North tend to share basic assumptions about science as rigorous knowledge, determination, rigor, truth, and reality and are deployed through an academic canon. Northern epistemologies have contributed to converting knowledge into a "hegemonic way of representing the world as one's own and of transforming it according to one's own needs and aspirations," which ultimately produced a Global North imperial domination of the world.[4] The story of how the Global North invaded the Global South presents a collision of epistemologies and an intellectual assault on cognitive justice. It is important to note that because the Global South is a political designation (as opposed to strictly geographic), Indigenous communities in the Northern Hemisphere are part of the Global South.

The very core of this chapter centers on the question of what counts as knowledge and who decides, and how it is maintained. Universities represent a key component of the verification process of constituting knowledge that is reified. There is a feedback loop or spiral of knowledge development. The process of how that spiral developed is part of understanding human societies, their corresponding relational complexities, and the rigid view of what is included in the canon within the world of formal education. Stepping away from the rigidity of formal education with regard to what constitutes knowledge, we intentionally take a broad, inclusive, and ecological perspective. Knowledges are intertwined and have varying degrees of knowability. Our point is that human understanding is interdependent with nature, other forms of human understanding, and even divine understanding. The possible worlds that extend out of those constellations may be as numerous as the stars, which limits human ability to know and understand.

In the human arrangement of what is knowable, a key ingredient enters our social worlds to organize knowledge—namely, the establishment of power. The hierarchy of knowledge organized by power is then legitimized into the world through a series of conventions and institutions which then can signal the weight of the knowledge, so that members of a society can use less of their time and energy scrutinizing the information and simply accept it as legitimate. The fruit born as a result of this hegemonic root system includes the development of research methods, the social construction and philosophies of science, the ways in which communities are designed around information (e.g., scholarly societies), and ultimately the institutions themselves that produce and reproduce knowledge creators (professors and researchers), distributors (journals and books), and credentials (degrees). All of these are the source and sustenance for continued legitimation of knowledge. This reality locates universities, in both historical and contemporary settings, toward the center of knowledge production.

Knowledge that exists and is formed outside the Western science canon (and therefore outside formalized academic parameters) is often not considered knowledge—at least in the formal sense of the word. Historically, other knowledge producers and monitors have been churches, monasteries, spiritual leaders, governments, civic leaders, independent researchers, scholarly societies, and think tanks. Universities have become massified, more uniform, and ubiquitous through increased student bodies, global recognition, and global rankings. These forces have converged in a way that positions universities as the most central social units to function as the core of knowledge production and monitoring.

For a tragic example of these forces of knowledge, consider how the early founder of anthropology and ethnology, Franz Boas, set out from Germany to northern Canada in 1883 to study Native people's perceptions and hunting habits. He took meticulous notes, went on harrowing journeys, learned enough of the local language and customs to navigate the region, and created social bonds to achieve his goals—scientific reports of the highest rigor. Upon arriving on Baffin Island, he enslaved a few people for free labor and conveyed a position of expertise as a medical doctor (even though his PhD was in physics). The people he attempted to treat became infected with diphtheria, and it ravaged the community with a high death count. Boas reflected in his journal on whether or not this was his fault.[5] This "study" became foundational to his career as he went on to become a professor at Columbia University in the United States and engage in debates about the degree to which race is biological and hierarchical. Though he was considered progressive in many issues of identity and justice, his career was built upon the people and communities who were harmed by his work.

When Indigenous knowledge and the sciences of First Peoples are systematically excluded, othered, demeaned, or categorized as something other than knowledge, the issues of cognitive justice and its implications become more evident. When ancestral knowledge is present in the bodies of students and young scholars and is systematically discounted, the display of White Western knowledge continues to masquerade as neutral, objective, and superior.

A Brief University History

In the preceding chapters we introduced some of the fruit of science and research that traveling Whiteness brought through the roots of White diasporic movement from Europe to the "new world," ultimately embodied in the institution of the modern university. The contemporary Western university is globalized and diffused through competition, rankings, and scholarly gatekeepers like journals and publishing companies. The university is quite distinct from some ancient centers of learning which were more epistemologically inclusive and expansive than the accepted contemporary parameters. When scholar settlers like Boas began to study groups of people, the accepted organization of human history at that time followed stages of development using the categories "savagery, barbarism, and civilization," put forth by J. W. Powell in his 1885 address to the Anthropological Society of Washington.[6] The artificial separations and stages served to disregard existing forms of knowledge and instruction. From an ecological knowledge viewpoint, the loss of language or knowledge is more akin to losing a plant or animal species in our ecosystem. The ecosystem suffers a loss of perspective and contribution to a larger view of humanity.

Universities and their formality and codification have played a role in this process. Consider the following historical summary of universities:

> All advanced civilizations have needed higher education to train their ruling, priestly, military, and other service elites, but only in medieval Europe did an institution recognizable as a university arise: a school of higher learning combining teaching and scholarship and characterized by its corporate autonomy and academic freedom. The Confucian schools for the mandarin bureaucracy of imperial China, the Hindu *gurukulas* and Buddhist *vihares* for the priests and monks of medieval India, the *madrasa* for the mullahs and Quranic judges of Islam, the Aztec and Inca temple schools for the priestly astronomers of pre-Columbian America, the Tokugawa *han* schools for Japanese samurai—all taught the high culture, received doctrine, literary and/or mathematical skills of their political or religious masters, with little room for questioning or analysis. Only in Europe from the 12th century onwards, did an autonomous, permanent, corporate institution of higher learning emerge and survive, in varying forms, down to the present day.[7]

The subtle dismissal of ancient forms of knowledge is one indicator of how knowledge supremacy becomes tied to region, culture, and race.

By way of brief summary, table 1 shows a select number of institutions of higher learning. The division in the middle highlights the origin point of the generally accepted origin of the modern university. Though the list in table 1 is condensed, the bifurcation between the left and the right columns highlights a prevalent approach to thinking about what counts as a knowledge producing/diffusing institution. Our intent is to critically examine the Eurocentric university model (right column), and to acknowledge and embrace the existence of profound knowledge that predated European universities.

Background

Understanding the role of universities as carriers and distributors of knowledge requires an understanding of the role of classification.

> Codified knowledge and higher education have always been, in one respect, essentially global. From their beginning in India, they derived their meaning and value from the movement of ideas and people between place-bound centers

Table 1
University Timeline[a]

Edubba House of Wisdom—Sumeria—3500 BCE	University of Bologna—Italy—1088 CE
Shangyang Higher School—China—2200 BCE	University of Paris—France—1150 CE
	University of Oxford—England—1167 CE
Takshashila University—Pakistan—600 BCE	University of Cambridge—England—1209 CE
	University of Salamanca—Spain—1218 CE
Mouseion at Alexandria—Egypt—Undetermined origination date	University of Coimbria—Portugal—1290 CE
	University of Heidelberg—Germany—1386 CE
Plato's Academy—Greece—387 BCE	University of St. Andrews—Scotland—1412 CE
Nalanda University—India—400 CE	
	National Univ. of Mexico—Mexico—1551 CE
University of Salerno—Italy—800 CE	Harvard University—USA—1636 CE
University of Magnaura—Constantinople—848 CE	Medical Academy of Salvador—Brazil—1808 CE
University of Qarawīyīn—Morocco—859 CE	University of Sydney—Australia—1851 CE
Al-Azhar University—Egypt—988 CE	University of Otago—New Zealand—1869 CE
Temple of Literature—Vietnam—1076 CE	Univ of the Cape of Good Hope—S. Africa—1873 CE

[a] List compiled from various university websites, histories, and publications including Perkin, 2007, and Sintayehu Kassaye Alemu, "Meaning, Idea and History of University/Higher Education: Brief Literature Review," *FIRE: Forum for International Research in Education* 4, no. 3 (2018).

of learning... The first of the medieval European universities was Bologna founded in 1088 for the study of Roman law. It was followed by more universities in Italy; by the University of Paris, which joined theology and philosophy; and later by Oxford. The first institutions were replicated across major cities within each culture in a wave of imitation. Thus began the mimetic pattern of development that still drives higher education and that embedded its differing forms within each regional domain.[8]

The preceding quote by Simon Marginson hurriedly summarizes the function and history of universities, and the allusion to India could discount all university centers of learning that preceded the Western European model. Then, moving on to discuss Bologna, Italy, Paris, and Oxford, Marginson identifies the model of the "first" institutions that were "replicated" in a wave of "imitation." The implicit point echoes Phillip Altbach's statement that "throughout the world, regardless of ideology, economic system, or historical circumstances, a variation of the Western university model predominates."[9] This functional, pragmatic, and seemingly objective statement about the current status of university models may appear neutral on the surface. From a root perspective, it invalidates and decontextualizes that which preceded this Western model. Marginson writes, "All the great centers of learning founded before Al-Azhar were destroyed," but then he added another explanation for the destruction by stating, "They ran out of the conditions of existence that sustained them."[10] What could it mean to run out of the conditions of existence?

As outlined in chapter 1, the tools of invasion have overlapping functions and influence, and their connection to a colonial dictation of academic models is profound. The combination of power and knowledge links the tools of invasion together, and the university is an institutional model for curating and codifying knowledge used in power. To understand the role of the university in relation to the knowledge-power constellation, academic communities need an excavation, an unearthing of the architectures of knowledge that seem to be settled and immovable. Reflecting on the role of mapping in the eras of discovery, conquest, and colonization, Piya Chatterjee and Sunaina Maira twist this orientation for a different account of universities as carriers of White dominance. Using the term "imperial cartographies," they write that "empires of knowledge rest on the foundation of racial statecraft, militarized science, and enduring notions of civilizational superiority," and these cartographies can help map the "research methods and scholarly theories" and their relationship to conquest.[11]

Claims of scholarly neutrality, along with the construction of concepts like savage, barbarous, primitive, and brutes, "helped create the very scaffolding of European and later US imperial cartographies."[12] Put differently, the dominant form of the university is not only complicit but is also central to cataloging and certifying forms of knowledge that support empire. Through relationships with scientific societies and the training of elites for bureaucracy, universities ultimately produce knowledge and ideology to underwrite conquest and dominance. We take the position that knowledge is everywhere, but that universities have played a role in putting boundaries around some knowledge and knowledge production such that it appears to exist only within the "rigorous" walls of the academy and ivory tower. The inability to see that knowledge and understanding exceeds the narrow-minded constructions of the Western world is to recreate oppressions.

Boaventura de Sousa Santos expresses the cartographies of oppression through the categories of Global North and Global South. These are political, not geographical, locations expressed in the Global North through "capitalism, colonialism, patriarchy, and all their satellite oppressions."[13] Those humiliated and degraded by these oppressions are in the Global South—although Santos asserts, "We are not victims. We are victimized and offer resistance. We are many and we use our new learning in very different ways."[14] Linking back to science and knowledge in the tools of invasion, our perspective emerges from Santos's construction of ecologies—specifically the ways in which the monoculture of Western science and knowledge discredits the possibility of knowledge outside the Western university's narrow and linear constructions of rigor. Santos's repeated position that there can be no global social justice without global cognitive justice is at the core of understanding ecologies of knowledge in opposition to monocultures. Santos further expands on the idea of the "global" by explaining that globalization is really a "local condition" that succeeds in "extending its reach over the globe" and then designates competing forms or conditions as "local." In this way, globalization and its discourses in knowledge are the narratives told by the "winners." It is a history that is the fruit of power; but there is "no global condition for which we cannot find a local root."[15]

As a final note on the background of globalization, knowledge, and power, the issue of race is often not fully considered in academic and political discussions. We build on the stance that "the complexity of contemporary global processes can never fully be grasped without a deep understanding of the historically-specific and dynamic ways race has ... [been] constituted by global transformations."[16] The "theft of history" is the story of how the past is conceptualized and presented according to Western Europe and imposed on the rest of the world. This imposition came with the claim of having invented a range of "value-laden institutions, such as democracy, mercantile capitalism, freedom, individualism ... The theft of history is not only one of time and space, but of the monopolization of historical periods."[17] A problem with the accumulation of knowledge is the European categorization and structure that defined knowledge parameters. This is true for many fields of knowledge that are housed by universities. We will focus on history/philosophy, medicine/science, and social science/statistics.

History/Philosophy

There is a mutually reinforcing conundrum that happens in relationship to the history of any discipline, but especially that of philosophy, which is often a tour confined to Western philosophy. Because we are considering history, globalization, and knowledge production with a racial lens, we see the categorization and codification of knowledge as uniquely linked. The origin of the history of race is debated, some linking it to Enlightenment science to justify enslavement, and others placing it with the beginnings of capitalism transitioning out of feudalism in the 1500s. Still others situate it even earlier in history but are critiqued for implementing a contemporary racial lens in periods that did not use the same categories. A salient point here is that all of these moments in history (and others not named) have contributed to the creation of race. Ibram X. Kendi notes how Puritan rationales for racial hierarchy and White superiority can be linked back to Aristotle (384–322 BCE) and the idea that extreme hot and cold climates produced an inferior and darker people. Aristotle labeled Africans as having burnt faces and—because of their climate—as lacking the capacity for intellect, freedom, and self-government.[18]

There is a profound and often unexamined problem with the underlying assumption that the most significant and superior knowledge production began with the Greeks. In the fifth century BCE, before Aristotle was even alive, the comprehensive historian Herodotus wrote, "In fact, the names of nearly all the gods came to Hellas [Greece] from Egypt. For I am convinced by inquiry that they have come from foreign parts, and I believe that they came chiefly from Egypt... These customs, then, and others besides, which I shall indicate, were taken by the Greeks from the Egyptians."[19] In the preface of the book *Stolen Legacy: The Egyptian Origins of Western Philosophy*, a reviewer wrote that the course called "Western Civilization" on many college campuses should be named either creative writing or "the propaganda of European intellectual supremacy as an ideological foundation for world domination."[20] *Stolen Legacy* is a refutation of Eurocentric narratives and myths about Western philosophy, which became the foundation for the structure of race.

The excavation of Western philosophy is an extensive project—and it begins with an explanation of the Egyptian Mystery System, which, like the modern university, "was the center of organized culture and candidates entered it as the leading source of ancient culture."[21] A few key points that highlight the glaring issues with Greco- and Eurocentrism include the fact that Greeks emigrated to Egypt for the purpose of advancing their own education. This took place after the Persian invasion of 525 BCE, and it continued until Greeks eventually took possession of Egypt when Alexander the Great invaded and occupied Egypt in 333 BCE. The prize possession was all of its intellectual resources, now appropriated by the Greeks with the claim of having "created" the cities, libraries, and intellectual centers, though they had only converted the fabric of knowledge that was already in place. In fact, Egyptian culture survived insofar as it was co-opted by the Greeks. The mystery temples and schools were maintained until edicts from Theodosius and Justinian in the fourth and sixth centuries CE closed them.[22]

The Greeks did not bring culture and learning to Egypt; they found it there and absorbed it, then settled in the land that produced the knowledge. Key moments in this line of critique include the history of Pythagoras, who traveled to Egypt for education from priests, learned their language and mysteries, and even brought them tokens of gratitude. He learned about medicine and geometry, including the properties of a right triangle, and showed his gratitude for this Egyptian knowledge that was bestowed on him. By way of another example, books attributed to Aristotle's authorship have a distinct association with Egyptian origins following the pillage of the royal library. The comparisons between the Mystery System and the lists of writings attributed to Aristotle show the origin of his thoughts. In these ways, the Greeks "stole the legacy of the African continent and called it their own."[23]

Like the Greek appropriation of Egyptian philosophy, the history of Africa has often been constructed by anthropologists with their own ethnology, histories, and classifications of peoples shaping their theoretical framework.[24] In both history and philosophy, this tradition still continues in the contemporary academic setting. Immanuel Kant (1724–1804), for example, considered by many to be one of the most influential Western philosophers, treated race as a scientific category and posited a racist hierarchy with White at the top. This tradition asserts and implies that Chinese, Indian, African, and Indigenous people are "congenitally incapable of philosophy."[25] These knowledges exist in the Western academic canon, and because they conceal their origins, deny status to other knowledges, and are preserved in the modern university, they perpetuate epistemicide and White dominance. History and philosophy are core disciplines and subject areas for undergraduate and liberal arts curriculums, and a doctorate of philosophy in any subject is considered the highest degree attainable.

Science/Medicine

Many forms of knowledge exist and have existed in ways that can be described as scientific, including natural philosophy, mathematics, and astronomy. Each of these, and many more, predates the emergence of the medieval European university and the Scientific Revolution that followed in the sixteenth century. Sources of knowledge and power have been competing for explanatory power and social status in all known human history. As the contemporary form of Western scholarship began its trajectory, the signal of knowledge was accompanied by the saying "according to science" or "most scholars agree," which replaced the declaration "thus saith the Lord."[26] The Western European Scientific Revolution was accompanied by new exploration, conquest, expanding centers of learning, and religious tumult during the period of the Reformation.

At the core of the tools of invasion that were deployed during this revolution was a vision of conquest. The project of modern science was to somehow escape from religious explanations and to organize society with a linear timeline and an imperial charter.[27] Science derives its explanatory power from conceptual claims to empirical, neutral, secular, and objective knowledge, all of which signal rigor in the highest form of knowing.

Britain had learned to leverage the strategic value of academies during its wars over territory, trade routes, and people. Universities including Oxford, Cambridge, St. Andrews, Glasgow, Aberdeen, Edinburgh, and Trinity were all tapped for resources and ideas during these wars. Students from Oxford paused their studies during English civil wars from 1642 to 1651, and universities facilitated colonial campaigns on behalf of England in Scotland and Ireland.[28] In addition, the Royal Society, the first scientific institution in England outside of the university, began in 1660 for the purpose of advancing experimental science with a royal charter from Charles II. Members of the Society met at Gresham College and began efforts to understand foreign countries and their inhabitants:

> Between 1660 and 1700, largely through the energetic efforts of Henry Oldenburg, the Society developed a widespread system of contacts, including European travelers, ambassadors, and colonists in foreign countries, to gather information needed to construct what Bacon called a natural and experimental history, and the request for information nearly always included questions about skin color. The passages on skin color in travel narratives began to be built according to the Society's design, in which writers debated the possible causes and often provided their own view... However, by the end of the century, the number of sets of queries were significantly reduced, and conversations about the issue at the meetings of the Society focused on black Africans.[29]

Though ideas of race emerged in other ways and in other time periods, including with the ancient Greeks, the connection of race to science, the slave trade, colonialism, and government elevated it to the view of the public. Attention to race in the Royal Society is an example of how knowledge production harnessed colonialism and science to direct attention to skin color and the advancement of the idea that race was an inherent trait.

Queries about skin color contributed to the development of the experimental method, and naturalists used this opportunity to improve their abilities. As a primary activity, the Royal Society sent out questionnaires about skin color so that English travelers could use the experimental method as a way to negotiate their relationships with other people. Emerging from the society was Robert Boyle's work "Experiments and Considerations Touching Colors" in 1664, which is considered a foundational study in empiricism. Boyle's focus on colors is valued in "the history of optics because it affirmed accurately that objects are seen as white because they reflect all light, and objects are seen as black because they absorb all light."[30] In addition to supporting Boyle's work on light, the society facilitated connections between travelers' reports, climate theory, and a new discourse on the causes of skin color that paved the way for increasingly racialized models of understanding the world.

In 1677, Royal Society member William Petty created a hierarchical scale of humanity in which he located Guinea Negroes at the bottom. In 1683, Increase and Cotton Mather founded colonial America's first formal intellectual group, the Boston Philosophical Society, which was modeled after London's Royal Society.[31] In New England, the origins of universities came with hundreds of Cambridge, Oxford, and Trinity alumni who arrived within the first twenty-five years of the settlement. The first colleges, including Harvard and William and Mary, were used as weapons of conquest of Indigenous peoples and were beneficiaries of African enslavement.[32] All of this contributed to the machinery of the Western scientific revolution that used race as a central feature of the structure.

Benjamin Franklin founded the American Philosophical Society in Philadelphia in 1743, also modeled after the Royal Society and the first association since the Boston society discontinued only four years after it began. The scientific revolution gave way to what came to be known as the Enlightenment in Britain and the colonies in America. During this time, racist ideas promoted discrimination by rationalizing disparities and targeting those enslaved as a problem people. Scientific categories and classifications expanded rapidly and repeated the notion of White as enlightened and desirable and Black as ignorant and undesirable. These ideas on race were the notions presented to Franklin's society and consumed by Thomas Jefferson, who would become the "preeminent American authority on black intellectual inferiority," as presented in his book *Notes on the State of Virginia*.[33]

Society members, students, and practices in colonial North America continued to craft a science to justify enslavement. The science generated continued claims of superiority:

> They did not abandon the search for truth, they redefined truth. Atlantic intellectuals had deployed science to prove the prophecies of the Bible, and now, with similar vigor they pursued the visible and manifest truths of the material world. Race did not come from science and theology, it came to science and theology. Racial ideas were born in the colonial world and the brutal and deadly processes of empire building. Science and theology deferred to race, twisting and warping under the weight of an increasingly popular and sweeping understanding of human affairs that tied the social fates of different populations to perceived natural capacities. Atlantic intellectuals operated under social and economic constraints that limited and distorted the knowable. The greatest accomplishments of the Enlightenment occurred within the inhumane and destructive realities of colonialism.[34]

The science of human races developed when the globe had been explored, peoples had been investigated by scientists, and theologies and theories had been tested. The science of race flourished with the growth of comparative anatomy.³⁵

As universities and medical schools categorized and codified knowledge, the growth of the discipline of anatomy required a set of specimens in order to verify their own legitimacy. In the case of Atlantic colleges, merit was measured by the possession of human remains including skulls, skeletons, and skins, which provided an advantage in an increasingly competitive educational market.³⁶ The beginning of American medical science corresponded with anatomy and the study of race. Biological perspectives on race became universally acknowledged and were compared to the certainty of the differences in sex. In 1811, Dartmouth Medical School moved into a building where the basement was piled with human bones. The college had been one of the largest enslavers in the colony, and state officials had buried their enslaved in the college cemetery. This became a resource for the medical college, which in colonial North America was literally "founded on the bodies of the poor and subjected."³⁷

Universities and academies for science circulated, codified, and dominated the study of race in anatomy, medicine, history, and anthropology. Colonial travels and conquests provided much of the observation and evidence, and the exchange of knowledge between British academies and America transmitted the information. For example, Scottish education influenced the American science, but at the University of Edinburgh, Scots were a minority of the student body, outnumbered by American students who came to generate "much of the new scholarship on medicine, pharmacology, and disease in the colonial world."³⁸ As Atlantic slavery "underwrote the production of knowledge, it distorted the knowable."³⁹

All of this biological and medical science produced a racial determinism in scientific discourse. In 1850, Robert Knox, a graduate of the University of Edinburgh, published *The Races of Men*, which outlined a kind of biological destiny that differed for Saxons, Celts, Jews, and the dark races of the world.⁴⁰ His accounts were influential for biological determinists, who established the foundation of social policies in another wave of race and social science. Like history and philosophy, the home for the development of this dominance and epistemic violence was the Eurocentric university—the model of which was planted around the world.

Social Science/Statistics

The transition of authority from religion to science and the accompanying role of race was depicted in the debates between monogenism and polygenism (both of which were anti-Black). Charles Darwin, a pioneer of evolutionary theories, was a monogenist committed to the idea that all humans derived from a single source. A relative of his, Francis Galton, went to medical school as well as Trinity and Cambridge to study math. They were an academic family, with relatives who were fellows in the Royal Society, as well as a religious family. Galton focused especially on counting and measuring variation and was influenced by his cousin's 1859 book *On the Origin of Species*. He focused his efforts of measurement on human variation, which made him an early leader in social statistics. Galton's translation of evolutionary ideas to humans and statistical logics would lead to the use of statistical analysis on human society.[41] His attraction to evolutionary theory and his statistical methodologies led to his racial theory of eugenics—biological explanations of racial variation and stratification.

Galton created the term "eugenics," based on the Greek term meaning "well-born." The purpose of eugenics was to breed suitable traits, or to offer optimal strains of blood a better chance of reproducing. Because biological traits were assigned to race (a social construct), the social classification of race allowed for ranking. Methodologically, experimental and inferential design "guided the development of research on race and biometrics in genetics," and "eugenic ideas were at the heart of the development of statistical logic."[42]

Following in Galton's footsteps was Karl Pearson, a British scientist who studied at Kings College and later became a professor at University College, London. There he was the first recipient of a Galton Eugenics Professorship where he stated, "No degenerate and feebleminded stock will ever be converted into healthy and sound stock by the accumulated effects of education, good laws, and sanitary surroundings. We have placed our money on environment when heredity wins by a canter."[43] Thus, the earlier influences of racialization culminated in eugenics, a race-based science. These ideas converged as seventy thousand individuals were involuntarily sterilized in the United States, and exponentially more in Germany in the 1920s and 1930s. The first international Eugenics Congress took place in London in 1912, garnering 750 participants, with follow-up congresses in 1921 and 1932.[44]

Eugenic organizations were founded in many countries and continents; but these ideas also influenced academic disciplines like anthropology, psychiatry, and sociology. The United States led the way with the passage of the first sterilization laws in the early 1900s. In only a couple of decades, half of the states passed involuntary sterilization laws, which primarily hurt poor, Black inmates of institutes for the "feebleminded." The birth of racial statistics provided scientific authority for the legitimation of racial inequality. The long history of racialization and the cooperation of universities in knowledge production about race has led to this malleable but potent construct in society: "Race is about an individual's relationship to other people within the society. While racial identification may be internalized and appear to be the result of self-designation, it is in fact a result of the merging of self-imposed choice within externally imposed context. When we forget or make slight of this point, social science becomes the justification for racial stratification ... Race is a social construct.

It is the international belief in race as real that makes race real in its social consequences."[45]

Statistical results do not reveal anything but a relationship between two or more variables. As a result, we cannot "learn from the data," because the data is generated by bias imbedded in the variable. Race is not an objective measurement and neither is intelligence, but both were born in the eugenics movement. They reveal a logic and a foundation whereby a researcher attempts to understand society. White logic is the "context in which white supremacy has defined the techniques and processes of reasoning about social facts ... White methods are practical tools used to manufacture empirical data and analysis to support the racial stratification in society."[46] These tools have been under construction and in constant evolution for at least five hundred years, and they are clearly present in the university system of researchers entangled in disciplines committed to justifying this legacy of White supremacy.

Conclusion

Universities are undeniably sites of oppression and resistance. Sweeping claims that universities are liberalizing, progressive forces often overlook the neocolonial ideologies they perpetuate. In this way, efforts to decolonize the university are not evidence of a liberalizing force in society so much as the opposite when it comes to knowledge production and credentialing. There are many efforts to decolonize the curriculum and to decolonize the university. Because knowledge exists outside the university and predates the modern or colonized university, the strategy of decolonization should include a deep recognition of precolonial universities and other knowledge systems. In recognition of the deep anti-Black current that runs through the power-knowledge partnership, a deep understanding of history, philosophy, and science can expose the colonized logic systems and help determine a path for unlearning and relearning. The anti-Black racist sentiments that were present in and cooperative with the development of the scientific method, Enlightenment science, and more recently eugenics are so deeply intertwined with the roots of modern higher education that the process of disentangling the logic systems must be done with an acute awareness that there is no social justice without cognitive justice.

If curriculums and universities do not identify and address the anti-Black attitudes that disenfranchised the majority of the globe and their knowledge systems at the origin point of the modern university, then curriculums and universities will maintain those anti-Black and colonial logic systems by propping up the status quo. As Gloria Ladson-Billings writes, "The issue is not merely to 'color' the scholarship. It is to challenge the hegemonic structures (and symbols) that keep injustice and inequity in place. The work is not about dismissing the work of European-American scholars. Rather it is about defining the limits of such scholarship."[47] What is considered scientific knowledge has been made a legitimate center in global knowledge production, with universities as the center, and knowledge acquisition occurs through diffusion in the periphery in a neocolonial division of labor.

To continue contextualizing universities historically and geographically as carriers of White dominance, the three regional case studies presented in the following chapters will thoroughly examine the ways in which the Eurocentric and White dominant university model played an important role as a tool of invasion. Though ostensibly neutral, knowledge-producing institutions, universities have long served as a respectable cover for racist ideologies lying just below the surface. Even today, colonizing ideology exists undetected in academic departments throughout the world, perpetuating epistemicide and preventing of cognitive justice.

Part 2
Case Studies

Introduction

The concepts from Part I ultimately help to frame the three case studies in Part II. More specifically, we observe how the tools of invasion were applied, the connection between homeland and the diaspora, and ultimately the formation of universities as carriers and perpetuators of White dominance. The map in Figure 5 from chapter 1 shows the route of the First Fleet leaving from England to settle/invade Australia. The route taken by the fleet of ships mirrors the geography of our case studies. The continents of Africa and South America were the earliest sites of invasion, and our case studies took place primarily in South Africa and Brazil. Later, Oceania as a connected but spread-out set of islands came into the European colonial view. There, our case study focused primarily on Australia and Aotearoa/New Zealand. Figure 10 also demonstrates that key moments in the colonization of these regions occurred with similar trajectories.

In the structure of each case study, we borrow the framework and conceptual categories developed by Linda Tuhiwai Smith, examining three sequential periods: precolonial, colonial, and postcolonial. We have labeled these differently, however, so as not to recenter colonization. Thus, the precolonial period, or what we refer to as life before invasion, is a brief summary of remembering and imagining life before colonial settlements in each region. For the case study of Oceania, for example, we have opted to employ the word *mana*, which is an oceanic concept for spirituality and power, instead of "precolonial," to capture and preserve the lives before invasion. In each of the following chapters, we do not make an attempt at comprehensiveness so much as acknowledge that most of history, culture, and knowledge production took place prior to the colonial

Southern Africa	South America/ Brazil	Oceania
KhoiKhoi, San, Bantu	Tikuna (and 300+ other groups)	Maori, Hawaiian, Aboriginal
	30,000+ yrs. Land and ecosystem Interdependence	
1488 Dias Portuguese exploration	1481 African slave trade to Protugal	1520 Magellan names the "Pacific"
1662 Dutch East India Company claims Table Bay	1500 Cabral Portuguese exploration	1768 Cook voyages begin
1829 University of Cape Town est.	1549 Salvador est. as capitol	1788 British "First Fleet" lands in Australia
1866 University of Stellenbosch est.	1730 Gold and diamonds discovered	1840 Treaty of Waitangi in Aotearoa
1867 Diamonds discovered	1808 School of Surgery, Bahia est.	1845 Beginning NZ Land Wars
1899 Start of the Boer Wars	1822 Colonial independence for Imperial Brazil	1850 University of Sydney est.
1948 Start of the Apartheid regime under the Nationalist Party	1888 End of Slavery	1869 University of Otago, NZ est.
1959 University Education Act	1964 Military govt. est.	1901 White Australia Policy
1994 End of Apartheid policies	2002 Affirmative Action policies at universities	1942 Australian Independence
		1947 New Zealand Indepdendence

FIGURE 10 Timeline across three regions. Images by William Bradley: Rio Janeiro (1787), Cape Town (1787), and Botany Bay (1788). These watercolors are bound into Bradley's journal *A Voyage to New South Wales, 1786–1792*. Mitchell library, State Library of New South Wales.

segments we examine. These accounts are not meant to encompass all or minimize other historical events, but to highlight key events as they relate to the book's major themes about the immense importance of culture and knowledge that exists outside of the colonizing canon.

The colonial period, which we refer to as the invasion period, represents the bulk of each chapter, as we document the history of arrival by White European settlers and interrogate the various components and tools of invasion, including a cross-cutting theme of the White diaspora. This section addresses the role of universities and the application of colonialism and its contemporary consequences as carriers of global White supremacy.

The third and final section of each of the three case study chapters focuses on the postcolonial era, or what we frame as decolonialization, Africanization, or rematriation. The focus in these sections is intended to offer implications on indigenous knowledge systems within and beyond the university, as well as ongoing protests and resistance within the university and beyond. We reflect on how the very sites of decolonization, tertiary educational spaces, are in fact also hosts to perpetuating dominant knowledge systems that serve to displace, dispossess, delegitimate, or even eliminate the Indigenous student.

4

Dominant White Minorities and Invasion in Southern Africa

> In an age of multiple postcolonial conditions afflicting the African continent, an exploration of African indigenous knowledges remains key to the advancement of the African agendas on a global landscape.[1]

South Africa is home to the "Cradle of Humankind," a paleontological site near Johannesburg that is home to the greatest concentration of ancestral remains in the world. According to radiocarbon dating the bones are millions of years old and demonstrate both the length of human existence and the brevity of time that this history is knowable. In spite of this, the colonizing academic canon typically begins African history with the point of invasion. A recovery of the truly ancient history of Africa is essential in order to decolonize the land, the people, and the academy.

The first people group in the region of South Africa were the Khoisan—an ethnic group found in the Cape around the beginning of the first century CE. Khoisan is a term that represents two groups who shared the same ethnic and linguistic heritage. The San way of life was generally that of nomadic hunter gatherers, while the Khoikhoi were pastoral herders. There is some overlap of the lifestyles of these two groups. Starting around the third millennium CE, the Bantu expansion extended south from the northern Congo region. The eastern portion of the South African cape was inhabited by Xhosa people. The Bantu people may have arrived several hundred years after the Khoisan. The Zulu nation did not inhabit modern-day South Africa until the 1600s. The history of foraging, subsistence, and hunter-gatherer lifestyles that lasted for thousands of years highlights the relationship between the sustaining power of the land and the interdependence of the people and the land. It was this ingenuity and interdependence that enabled this place and these peoples to form the cradle of humanity.

Invasion Period

On the southern tip of the African continent, a variety of peoples settled and lived for tens of thousands of years prior to the arrival of European explorers, settlers, and colonizers. Even following the Europeans' exploitation of natural resources, their drawing of arbitrary lines into republics, and the independence of countries from their colonial powers, White identity played an ongoing role in places now known as Zimbabwe, Zambia, and South Africa. Colonization and the expansion of European invasion began in 1497, when Portuguese explorer Vasco da Gama purportedly landed on the coast of Natal on Christmas Day. Natal, a Portuguese word for Christmas, would be named and claimed Terra Natalis, and the Natal region would be occupied as a trading post in the mid-1500s.

The cape of South Africa also became a point of interest to the Dutch East India Company and other traders who established supply stops on trade routes. The Dutch East India Company was established in 1602, and in 1652, Jan van Riebeeck, representing the company, named and claimed Cape Town (or Kaapstad in Dutch) at Table Bay. Cape Town served primarily as a waystation for various ships that they sent to the East Indies through this trading hub. Disappointed with the lack of agricultural skills among the Khoisan, the Dutch imported their own farmers, known as the Boers (the Dutch word for farmers). Eventually some of the Dutch, many of whom were Calvinists who had been persecuted in Europe, stayed in the region and migrated away from the cape to the inland areas and farmed there. The chief identifying characteristic of many of the Dutch settlers who had been in the land for a long time was speaking Afrikaans (a derivative of the Dutch language). The British also settled there and officially annexed the Cape Colony in the early nineteenth century, setting up a conflict between the British elite and the rugged Dutch Boers. The cape was eventually populated by the English after a century of war and armed resistance known as the Kaffir Wars of 1779–1879. The Anglo-Boer Wars ended in the early twentieth century under a treaty that created the Union of South Africa, which included self-governing colonies of Afrikaners and others. The tenacity of the White Afrikaners is a profound example of the White diaspora mentality. When those with power can breed a victim mentality, they create a paradox of suffering.

After the Anglo-Boer Wars, English-speaking and Afrikaner White people came together under a unified idea—that Whites had the ability to express their culture differently, but that they needed to be unified to "withstand the threat of black domination" and that segregation would be a "permanent solution."[2] This unification characterized the transition from colonialism to apartheid, in which White Afrikaners combined the power of the common language as the means to communicate nationalist aspirations. Deeply rooted in the Afrikaner myth was the personification of oppression from elite Whites and the threat of Black natives. Throughout the colony, connections to the White English speakers were an imperial economic endeavor—most notably by Cecil John Rhodes, the imperialist mining magnate whose company founded the territory named Northern and Southern Rhodesia (now Zambia and Zimbabwe).

Deeply ingrained in a Christian nationalist ideology, the Dutch Reformed Church and its unique scriptural hermeneutics were shaped in large part by theologian and politician Abraham Kuyper (1837–1920). His Neo-Calvinist thinking and writing was adopted by many Dutch Reformed leaders who embraced Kuyper's notions of sphere sovereignty, a major tenet of the Kuyperian worldview that held that church, state, and societal institutions ought to be separated into distinct silos. This theological view, paired with a colorist and anti-Black racist worldview, led to the belief that each ethnic or racial group should maintain its own distinct national and spiritual identity.[3] The slogan "South Africa First" was an explicit Whites-only variety of nationalism that characterized the period leading up to apartheid. The purity of South Africa and a National Party was a code for racial purity and supremacy. Politician Daniël François "D.F." Malan drove much of the fear about a loss of national ideas and in 1948 was the first National Party leader to become prime minister. Prior to his life as a politician, he was a clergy member in the Dutch Reformed Church, which gave D.F. Malan the skills to leverage Afrikaner nationalism into a civil religion under the slogan "Believe in your God, Believe in your country, Believe in yourself."[4] This would remain the motto for the National Party through the 1960s.

White capitalist Christian ideologies came together to create a power block maintained by Afrikaner determination. So, apartheid policies took hold with the stated intention of allowing Black people to develop at their "own pace" as opposed to being subject to the "superior" educational settings for White people. The separate notions were facilitated most significantly through the church. The Dutch Reformed Church continued to collude with the government in a way that compromised its own stated ideals of sphere sovereignty to activate the inherent anti-Blackness of many White Dutch Christians in leadership in South Africa. In 1957, for example, the church accepted a prohibition against Black peoples attending churches in White areas. This was preceded by the 1949 Mixed Marriages Act, which prohibited marrying across races in an attempt to maintain racial purity. By the mid-1960s, most White citizens were in favor of apartheid policies, confirming a powerful overlap between the British economic and imperial approaches to race and the religious fervor of the Afrikaners.

From political oppression and death squads[5] to deep layers of intentional miseducation and misappropriation of religion, apartheid was devastating even beyond its official end in 1994.[6] The residual effects are still evident in the massive levels of inequality and debates about how to deal with a White market-dominant minority in a country that is now mostly governed by the Black majority. In the neighboring countries of Zambia and Zimbabwe as well, there remains a flavor of White dominance, although there have been some concrete moves to distribute unequal wealth resulting from colonization. The legacy of the White diaspora continues through two of the oldest universities, as well as other institutions, as they struggle with the legacy of their contributions to invasion and oppression while simultaneously hosting extensive discussions about the decolonization of their curriculums.

Higher Education and the University as Tools of Invasion

The initial apartheid policies of 1948 benefited both Afrikaners and Boers. English-speaking White minorities also benefited by proximity, but the imposition of oppressive policies was especially designed to lift the status of Afrikaners. Many official acts of government were passed in addition, such as the Mixed Marriages Act (1949), the Immorality Act (1947/1950), and the Group Areas Act (1950), which broadly impacted educational policies.

More specifically related to education were the Bantu Authorities Act (1951) and the Bantu Education Act (1953). Bantu was a name given to native ethnic groups to assist in prescriptive racial segregation of everything in society. The Bantu Education Act was labeled education that conformed to the needs of people who were not White, when in reality it was a miseducation to prepare students for a life of subservience and labor. Figure 11 includes a picture of H. F. Verwoerd and one of his quotes arguing for segregated schooling with an explicit racist ideology.

A critical education-related legislative decision occurred with the University Education Extension Act of 1959, an apartheid-era policy enacted by an all-White parliament. This effectively closed White universities to Black South

FIGURE 11 H. F. Verwoerd and his 1953 quote about the Bantu Education Act. (Photo by author.)

African students and created segregation policies for universities open to Black students. South African universities that taught in the Afrikaans language had already created barriers to integration and all but ensured that the student population would be White Afrikaners. The immediate impact of the policy was on non-White students who were already attending the universities of Cape Town, Witwatersrand, and Natal, which had more open admissions policies.

For institutions that had previously served many Black and other non-White students, such as the University of Fort Hare, where both Nelson Mandela and Robert Mugabe graduated, the university systematically deteriorated due to the Bantu Education Act and especially the University Education Extension Act.[7] Upon passage of the act, the government seized control of the University of Fort Hare and redesignated it to serve only Xhosa students, who were then to receive truncated and incomplete education in accordance with Bantu education policy. The minority party in parliament at the time, the United Party, objected to the law, as did a number of university professors and non-White students who signed petitions, issued statements, and marched in protest rallies. This legislation remained until the act was finally repealed in 1988.

The University of the Western Cape, located in a suburb of Cape Town and originally referred to as a "bush college," was established in 1960 by the South African government as a result of the Extension of University Education Act in 1959. The purpose of the "bush college" was to offer limited training for Black and Colored students to prepare for low-level civil service work and other positions within schools. The mostly White faculty were borrowed from Stellenbosch University, and instruction was delivered almost exclusively in Afrikaans.

The earliest inception point of academic endeavors of research and academia can be seen through the work documentation and record-keeping of European settler colonial invaders. They brought with them the European versions of these tasks, mostly because they were beholden to their commissioning bodies to report back on the progress they were making in "uninhabited" lands for the sake of king and country.

We argue that modern universities exist to codify the stories, cultures, and people who were already in existence. Only when they are named, claimed, and codified do they come into the gaze of the academy. Similar to White Europeans in other parts of the world, here the White settlers shared a belief in their natural superiority. This shared social Darwinism was an additional layer with Afrikaner Calvinists who believed that Black people were an inferior race, "destined by God to provide menial labor."[6] Afrikaner nationalism developed rapidly in the early twentieth century by pursuing White supremacy thorough discriminatory laws and separate structures. Things changed for the worst with the discovery of gold in 1886 on the Witwatersrand, and the discovery of diamonds in Kimberely in 1867. In the midst of all of the wars and land grabs among colonizing nations in the mid-1800s, settler colonials established a system of higher education in South Africa. Two of the oldest two universities in South Africa are the University of Cape Town, founded in 1829, and the Stellenbosch University, founded in 1885, both of which will be discussed in the following section.

University of Cape Town (UCT)

The University of Cape Town (UCT) was originally formed as South African College, a secondary school for boys, which was increasingly seen as a necessity as White settlers flocked to exploit the gold and diamond mining in the territory. As these endeavors increased, a demand for skilled knowledge in mining became increasingly essential; laboratories were created and departments of mineralogy and geology grew in enrollment and eventually led to UCT gaining status as a bona fide university. In honor of Queen Victoria's Diamond Jubilee in 1887, UCT decided to admit female students permanently to its campus.

University of Cape Town was established formally as a university in 1918, due in large part to private donations from benefactors like Julius Wernher, Alfred Beit, and Cecil John Rhodes, who made their fortunes by monopolizing the mining industries.[7] Alfred Beit, for example, made his millions from mining gold, silver, and diamonds. Kimberley, where the Kimberley Central Company relocated to mine diamonds, is where Beit met, hired, and befriended Cecil John Rhodes. Together they created many financial schemes to ensure control of the diamond-mining claims, including those of De Beers. Rhodes served as the public face and politician, while Beit privately played the role of strategist and financier.

Beit leveraged his fortunes to support sciences and other disciplines at various universities. At the University of Oxford, Beit donated funds to establish the Beit Professorship of Colonial History in 1905. Beit's endowment remains as a professorship in history, under the new title Beit Professorship of Commonwealth History. The post is held in conjunction with a fellowship at Balliol College, Oxford, where Cecil Rhodes bequeathed nearly £12 million in today's equivalent. The University of Cape Town moved to its current location in 1928 on land that Rhodes bequeathed to South Africa. Each time we walked onto the campus (see figure 12), the combination of the mountains, the Greek columns, the steps, and the history of the prestigious university impressed upon us the wealth and prestige of its founders.

Generous donations came from benefactors like mining magnate Julius Wernher, who with Beit combined for most of the ownership of all the diamond mines throughout Southern Africa through questionable business practices. As they became the barons of mineral-rich properties, they were occasionally referred to as "Randlords," as they drove up the value of the South African currency (the rand) due to soaring real estate prices. They not only gave generously to universities; they also privately financed several national political endeavors. Randlords like Rhodes, Beit, and Wernher were often blamed for the Anglo-Boer War of the late 1890s to the early 1900s. Wernher and Beit, along with a handful of others within the diamond syndicate, had firm

FIGURE 12 View of UCT. (Photo by author.)

control of diamond sales, pricing, and quality. Rhodes, Wernher, and Beit were often found in partnership on various profiteering ventures, land settlement, and other agricultural schemes. Wernher, Beit, & Co.'s efforts to secure increasing profits on a variety of financial and mining deals aligned with the political savvy and thirst for power and expansion evidenced by Rhodes in the late 1880s and through the early 1900s. Diamond syndicates, or investment trusts, were established by many of the mining tycoons, who served as directors of these syndicates and who were looking for quick profits from speculation in addition to running and maintaining legitimate and more profitable mines. These were unscrupulous men who made their fortunes in morally and ethically questionable ways. And yet having amassed their fortunes, they funneled some funds to ensure that universities like UCT would survive.

Associated with the self-image and the prestige was an immense amount of stress about admissions standards. One professor told us, "How can you admit students who can't pass the basic maths, who can't read the requisite works of literature, or construct essays with proper grammar? It wouldn't be fair to them." The faculty member was making reference to the age-old issue of "fit" in college admissions. The more acute issue, of course, is the fact that Black South Africans have been subject to intentional miseducation for decades—and in a postapartheid era, the gains in admission and hiring in elite places like UCT have been too slow. We saw signs posted around campus advertising discussions about racial topics as well as other pertinent issues like sexual assault. The White resistance to expanding was visible and audible, as well as groups articulating a vision for Africanizing as well as decolonizing the curriculum.

Stellenbosch University

A Dutch-style secondary school was first established in the town of Stellenbosch in 1685. Stellenbosch University (SU) emerged as a theological seminary of the Dutch Reformed Church in 1859. The Calvinist religion the church followed gave it a way to mythologize its history as God's chosen people, their migration across the country akin to the biblical Exodus from Egypt to the promised land.[8] The university's primary language of instruction and operation has been Afrikaans until recently, when increasing demands for diversity and protest have broadened the linguistic environment. The university initially had a hundred students and two faculty members: one in mathematics and natural sciences, and the other in classical literature. For a brief period, the Dutch university underwent a name change. In 1887 the institution was renamed Victoria College in honor of Queen Victoria's fifty-year celebration of her ascent to the British throne (also known as the Golden Jubilee). Victoria College's name was changed to Stellenbosch University in 1918 due in large part to a £100,000 donation by a local benefactor, Jan Marais. The intent was clear for the founders of SU, that tertiary education and scholarship would be reserved for the learned few who could read and write in Afrikaans. Indeed, Marais donated significant sums to ensure that Afrikaans language and culture would remain intact. We had the occasion to visit the Afrikaans Language Museum in Stellenbosch in 2018. The efforts to preserve the language, theology, and culture were remarkable and had no reference to any of the fruit of apartheid and other atrocities that stemmed from bad theology and extreme ethnocentrism and linguistic hegemony.

Stellenbosch University had long been considered the intellectual birthplace of the seat of Afrikaner ethnocentrism. The theology and political science curriculums and faculty served as academic incubators of apartheid ideology. Often referred to as the cradle of Afrikaner nationalism, Stellenbosch was the site of the original design for the Nationalist Party's version of apartheid, led in large part by Hendrik Verwoerd, who studied theology at the university and eventually became a professor in sociology. Later he would become prime minister from 1958 until his assassination in 1966.

Balthazar Johannes "B. J." Vorster served as the prime minister of South Africa from 1966 to 1978 and as fourth state president from 1978 to 1979. As minister of justice, Vorster was a key supporter of apartheid and oversaw the Rivonia Trial that ensured the life imprisonment of Nelson Mandela; and as prime minister he was the architect of the Terrorism Act, which led to the complete abolition of non-White political representation. Vorster entered SU to study law. In fact, six out of the seven South African prime ministers between 1910 and 1971 were students at SU. Moreover, Vorster served as SU's eighth chancellor. Stellenbosch University was also the site of the original design for the Nationalist Party's version of apartheid, and Verwoerd was one of its major architects. During his time at the university, he joined other professors in protesting the immigration of German Jews who were fleeing persecution from the Nazis. He also refined his views on the role of race in society and went on to serve in the Senate, then as minister of Native affairs, and eventually as prime minister. Key acts of apartheid were passed throughout his time holding public office.

The ideologies of racism, colorism, and colonialism were embodied and perpetuated by the administrators, faculty, and students in the early days through various disciplines of pseudoscience. Much of this was based on "the Curse of Ham" theology, which is a misinterpretation of Christian scripture that justifies the enslavement and subjugation of Black people as being ordained by God. The university played a significant role in contemporary apartheid practices in the 1950s–1990s. For example, under the Group Areas Act of 1950, an area known as Die Vlakte (Afrikaans for "The Flats") was declared a White Group Area, and thus many "colored" residents within the broader university neighborhood were forced to evacuate their homes. While a handful of examples of faculty dissent have been preserved, no record exists that SU itself protested the evictions. For nearly four decades, this forced segregation left SU isolated from its neighbors of color. Hilton Biscombe compiled a book, *In Ons Bloed*, that collected and documented the memories of members of this community. In 2007, the university dedicated the Lückhoff Secondary School building, once expropriated for the university during apartheid, back to the community as a gesture of reconciliation and transformation.

Stellenbosch has a very different feel from UCT. Similar notions of being elite exist in the university's culture; but because Afrikaans has been and is the primary language of instruction, there is an extra sense of White Afrikaner dominance there. This history is present in the language, architecture, curriculum, and even the proximity of the Dutch Reformed Church across the street. Several faculty members lamented to us, "It is very difficult that we are forced to publish in a second language, but so many journals are in English, it is the only way we can progress." During the time of the interview, the university was beginning to relax some of its strict language policies; but it was ironic thinking about Black South African students learning Xhosa and English, and then having to learn a third language, and to listen to faculty lament having to make considerations for English. Some of the students expressed that English actually represents a "language of resistance" at a place like Stellenbosch because of the power and history of Afrikaans.

Educational Colonization and Epistemic Erasure

We underscore here that in many parts of the world, such as on the continent of Africa, colonialism accompanied by European nationalism effectively and unilaterally declared all the knowledge systems that people had used and maintained for centuries to be unfit, primitive, irrelevant, and even evil. In government and education, Indigenous knowledge systems were replaced. Formally, this occurred through structures of law and policy; and informally, it occurred by way of an emerging self-hatred and internalized oppression among Indigenous peoples. Colonialism thus generated a Bantu education system yet also fostered a level of collective insecurity and self-doubt in dominated groups, which has led to the generational transfer of inadequacy beliefs and created false cognitive deficiencies in billions of people. South Africa operates at a deficit when learning does not include marginalized people. Decolonization is one way to describe the need to reeducate or rewrite narratives against the ongoing dominance of knowledge theft through education.

By disrespecting and erasing the heritage of Indigenous knowledge systems and by devaluing the underlying foundational constructs of ethical, social, and philosophical Indigenous systems, colonizers-turned-educators were able to successfully dominate groups, denying their right to a true sense of being through formal Westernized and colonialized ways of knowing. This in many ways became the ultimate form of epistemological theft and cognitive injustice. Colonizers effectively created an epistemology that left millions of Black and Colored South African students believing that the problem lay with them, in failing to see themselves in the curriculums.

Marginalized and colonized people in colonial South Africa felt hurt and disrespected as White European knowledge and epistemologies became increasingly official, standard, and natural. Variations of linguistic hegemony also appeared, as native tribal languages were not considered acceptable forms of communication; the accepted scholarly and academic voices then "naturally" appeared in the form of English or Afrikaans. Early White European colonial settlers observed and believed that the vast repository of knowledge produced by Indigenous people was primitive and therefore had little value and could even be harmful to Black Africans in their own development. Colonialism, together with European nationalism, intentionally and systematically dismissed and excluded these forms of knowledge through formal education systems. What counted as knowledge was decided by an externally imposed hegemonic system of validation and codification.

In many ways, this Eurocentric dominance continues in education today, because equity scholars have left unchallenged the assumption that there are transcendent truths that are independent of people and an underlying physical reality that is experienced in the same way by all people irrespective of their history, culture, and language. This hegemony in education is premised on the assertion that the European mode of thought has delved deeper into these "transcendent truths" and understands the physical world better than any other modes of Indigenous or local thought. All academic disciplines within the academy established by European imperialism erased native and Indigenous knowledge and replaced them with a construction of African realities that were rooted in faulty, anti-Black colonial anthropology.

Scholars in the academy were particularly violent in their epistemicide and notorious for their colorist, racially charged, and distorted views of African culture and people. Black Africans were largely portrayed by European colonizers as primal, uncivilized, soulless, immoral, and savage. The canonization of authors such as Joseph Conrad and his seminal work in 1902, *Heart of Darkness*, serve as fruit borne of the deep-seated anti-Black roots of imperialism. It continues to be dangerous to presume that Africans had no history, and that African culture maintained only a primitive existence until Europeans "discovered" the land and the people and led them toward true civilization. African peoples, of course, had existed and flourished long before colonial invasion, with a history of civilization predating any European imperialist period. African history and culture were documented and recorded, just as most civilizations have been over the millenniums.

The activism of Black South African students is not a new phenomenon, and in fact has a long history in the fight against racism and anti-Blackness in education. The Soweto Youth Uprising on June 16, 1976, was a historic moment and a turning point in the education system in South Africa at the height of apartheid. An estimated thirty thousand Black students led the protest. Their actions were met with police violence, and many students were brutally murdered. One of those children murdered that fateful day was 11-year-old Zolile Hector Peterson, a Black child who was shot and killed by the apartheid police. His lost life and the lives of countless others taken that day were not in vain; the Soweto Youth Uprising was the defining moment in the resistance against the imposition of the Afrikaans language on Black South African students. Youth Day continues to be a public holiday commemorating the death of Zolile Hector Peterson and the roughly seven hundred other children who were victims of police violence. We could feel the presence and consciousness around that violence as we observed the memorial in Soweto and spoke with residents about their memories.

In March of 2015, a group of student activists began to protest on the campus of the University of Cape Town. This movement eventually spread throughout the region, and other campuses began to organize and protest as part of what became known as the #RhodesMustFall campaign. We visited the country in the aftermath of the student demonstrations. Part of the protest focused on the propagation of a figure like White South African diamond magnate Cecil Rhodes, the benefactor who bequeathed large sums to finance scholarships and sponsored the erection of many buildings on college campuses and other facilities throughout the region. He had been critiqued publicly for his settler colonial and White supremacist ideologies. In fact, his writings reveal a deep-seated racial national pride, and the expansion of educational institutions aligned with his goal for racial purity and prosperity. In *Confession of Faith*, Rhodes wrote in 1877 the following thoughts on the "master" race:

> I contend that we are the finest race in the world and that the more of the world we inhabit the better it is for the human race. Just fancy those parts that are at present inhabited by the most despicable specimens of human beings what an alteration there would be if they were brought under Anglo-Saxon influence, look again at the extra employment a new country added to our dominions gives. I contend that every acre added to our territory means in the future birth to some more of the English race who otherwise would not be brought into existence.[9]

A few White South African interviewees argued that Rhodes was not a White supremacist but merely a "man of his time." We find this type of thinking to be problematic as it allows supremacist and racist beliefs to be justified. It reinforces White hegemony. This type of thinking excuses the complicity of the architects of a racist South African higher education system. Alternatively, a few proponents of the Rhodes Must Fall movement stated that it served as a call for direct action in order to redress the "racist and unequal vision" that has manifested within South African universities.

The campus protest resulted in a quick win, with the removal of a large statue of Cecil Rhodes from the University of Cape Town. A few of the White South African administrators we interviewed expressed their frustration with the newest manifestations of student outrage, saying that the primary issue moved beyond the removal of statues. They were more concerned with students who wished to rewrite history to meet their own desires. They likened Black and Colored UCT students to "your snowflakes in the United States," who lack a deeper appreciation for the history of the country. They lamented openly with us and expressed frustration, assuming that we as White faculty members understood their pain (this particular interview was with Collins who is White and Jun who is Korean American).

They expressed disappointment in the move to expose institutional racism at South African universities. The idea of decolonizing tertiary education was anathema to some White administrators who, while certainly against apartheid and supportive of the regime change, felt threatened or alarmed by both the amount and pace of change that student protesters were seeking. A similar sentiment was posted in public spaces with posters that included the moniker #IsUCTFree and statements like, "Yes, Black people can be racist too" and "When did freedom become unfashionable?" The resistance to exposing White supremacy through Africanizing the curricula and addressing issues of access and affordability clearly stoked more feelings of White supremacy.

On one particularly rain-soaked morning in Cape Town, we ventured to a local university to meet with a professor who identifies as a Black South African. She moved south at a young age from Zambia, and thus was in possession of a South African ID, which her parents had applied for when she was young. She shared how her South African ID was a source of both pride and frustration. On the one hand, it was a cherished and coveted credential that led to employment opportunities, given the oversaturated job market in South Africa. On the other hand, she recognized the anti-Blackness, colorism, nativism, and xenophobia found among Black South Africans as well. She shared about her struggles with mistreatment and alienation for being an outsider to Black South African cultures and communities: "I'm very much a Black person, and I'm very much for pro-Blackness. But you also know that your Blackness amongst the locals is also limited because they don't really identify with you completely. But you still share certain customs, values; things like this make you an outsider among Black colleagues."

She also admitted to her own racial animus toward some Black South African colleagues. Given some of her education and upbringing outside of South Africa, she was told by White South African colleagues that she has a different accent, one that she was told was more articulate and professional than other Black South African educators. She found herself agreeing with her White colleagues, and she looked down on the unprofessional attire, comportment, and speaking styles of her fellow Black colleagues. This dual tension of colorism, exclusion, and nativism among Black scholars reveals the complex residual effects of colonial anti-Blackness. "The more polished you are, the more opportunities you will have to attend better schools, live in better communities and better social groups," she told us. "This is true today, in postapartheid South Africa."

This faculty colleague also shared about inequities beyond but not excluding race and addressed the economic realities that continue to fall on ethnic lines. She is not completely convinced that political power is no longer with White people, as a lot of Black people who are in politics may also be funded by some White elites. Colonization is ongoing, even with the end of apartheid. Afrikaners were not ready for change and still are not. Perhaps they never will be. They continue the fight to keep their homelands and to preserve their heritage culture and language, as evidenced by the Afrikaans Language Museum and other institutions where we conducted site visits. Yet for Black South Africans in a postapartheid, postcolonial South Africa, one means of restoring some dignity might come through the land. This is land that was stolen from them, land that they were denied through forced removals, war, and racist policies. This is land and property that many still do not possess. With the increased visibility of Black South Africans in politics, education, and other spheres of society, there may be an increase of Afrikaner flight (e.g., White South African farmers who were welcomed by the Australian government).

Decolonization in South Africa: A Way Forward

Long-held imperial assumptions are increasingly coming under intense interrogation by the current generation of students, who rightly believe that they are not here to adapt to the world as it stands, but to act and to change it become more just, equitable, and inclusive.

The call for decolonized education found renewed impetus during the #FeesMustFall movement that received greater attention starting in 2015 when the call for free education was blended in with a call for decolonized education. Discussions and debates that ensued have been broad and diverse; they have addressed the complexities that need to be embraced on the journey toward an understanding of what it means to undo colonialism within the South African higher education system.

This belief is often expressed in revolutionary terms and as an all-consuming, all-encompassing vision of decolonization. One broad definition of decolonization that emerged through the student protest movement is "the removal of all unjust systems such as patriarchy, racism, and capitalism in society and the restructuring of society to reflect African systems," as one scholar-activist stated. Increasing numbers of White South African educators and politicians fear that some of these aspirations will lead to the arbitrary and violent overthrow of policies and structures, and resistance comes in the form of criticisms of a lack of tolerance in the effort toward change and progress. In particular because aspirations do not come with clear and measurable implementation plans, the task of translating understandings of decolonization in operational terms for the purposes of teaching, learning, and the curriculum, presents manifold challenges.

An ongoing debate preoccupying some African scholars surrounds the question of how to write the colonial period into African history. On one side, some scholars seek to minimize the colonial impact given the long history of the African continent, which has survived multiple forms of attack and invasion. On the other side, some scholars argue that while comparatively brief, colonization has forever altered the course for African knowledge systems and approaches that seek to elucidate the unending import of the colonial situation.

Scholars of African studies Olajumoke Yacob-Haliso, Ngozi Nwogwugwu, and Gift Ntiwunka have posited that African scholars have helped frame and juxtapose these two views.[10] One school of thought views colonialism as merely a brief period of imperial subjugation that, given the historical arch of African nations, does not significantly disrupt the long-term future of Africa in its social, academic, and cultural life. The second and alternative view of colonization is that while the colonial invasion period was relatively brief, lasting less than a century, the damage is long-lasting, extensive, and irreparable. The intense exploitation and oppression of settler colonialism and its epistemicide have been disruptive enough to displace academic and social institutions. Any efforts toward a re-ordering of cultural, political, social, religious, and economic life will fall short of full restoration, as nothing was left undamaged by the imperialism and erasure by White European invaders. The roots of this colonialism may continue to bear unintended fruit in South Africa's future.

As South Africa makes the slow, painful turn away from the colonized educational practices of the last several hundred years, it must ask itself a challenging question: what is the difference between decolonizing and Africanizing an education system? Many South African scholars such as John Volmink and others have been actively pursuing answers to this question, and their work serves the broader community well in seeking corrective measures moving forward.

In an interview with one scholar-activist who is working toward systemic change, he projected that what is needed most in higher education is "a replacement of arbitrary and violent alteration of policy by students with institutionally channeled change, ordered by reasoned persuasion and informed consent. The call for the decolonization of the South African education must be mainstreamed." Although the call for decolonization originates from the Fallist Movement, the call is for the greater localization and Africanization of knowledge. The intent is rooted in the promotion, celebration, and normalization of Indigenous literacies and knowledge. A critical analysis, social cohesion and identity, and the spirit of *ubuntu* (humanity) are traits that must be securely rooted within the new global space.

During the colonial period, the colonizing of the mind was made possible through a curriculum that was both Eurocentric and designed to underdevelop and exclude Black people. Colonization of the mind has become a more subtle and lasting manifestation of colonialism. Education was used as a strategic tool to maintain and reproduce colonial attitudes. Currently, the curriculums across institutions of higher learning in South African universities are still heavily Eurocentric, with little focus on Africa more broadly and South Africa specifically. A conspicuous absence of Indigenous knowledge, and the marginalization of Indigenous languages and ways of knowing, continue to plague the postcolonial South African higher education system. A Black South African scholar summarized the future to us in the following way: "While recognizing that there is currently a lack of common understanding of what is meant by decolonization of knowledge and curricula, and how it should be implemented and driven within the context of the classroom and in policy, we need to unpack the concept of decolonization of education and what it means in South African context, assess its impact on the state of education in South Africa, and possibly, sketch a roadmap that befits the South African educational landscape." This sentiment aligns with what other scholars have urged: namely, the examination of scholarship and the vigorous questioning of the continued dominance of White, colonial, even racist scholars, tropes, archives, and knowledges in the study of African peoples.[11]

Scholar Mahmood Mamdani recalled a time in 1998 during a lecture in postapartheid South Africa when he posed this question for the audience: when does a settler become a native? Never. This is the answer he offered then and continues to believe now. The native, Mamdani argues, is the creation of the settler state, and "the native is the settler's invented other . . . the settler and the native are joined; neither can exist in isolation. Should you destroy one, the other would cease to exist."[12]

Mamdani's interpretation confirms our own findings of the series of decision-making processes in a postapartheid South Africa, which are telling of the fundamental problem with ongoing settler colonial ways of thinking. Our original premise of the White diaspora and anti-Blackness both among White and some Black educators reveals the ongoing challenge of decolonization efforts in South Africa. The fruits of White logic manifest themselves through the punishment of perpetrators for individual intentional and malicious crimes; most of the criminalized being Black South Africans. White logic further manifests through the creation of fabricated shared spaces, where former victim and former perpetrator together are expected to live peaceably together without harming one another. White logic keeps injustice at an individual level. This White logic consequently responds slowly or ignores outright the ongoing consequences of systemic injustices that have led to generational wealth and ongoing existence on prime properties for White people, and the decimation of a language, culture, and epistemologies for Black people.

Afrikaners who once championed the idea of apartheid later became part of the movement against it. As South Africa attempted to decolonize, it attempted to eliminate colonial distinctions between settlers and natives, having them join the same political communities. Settlers suddenly emerged as immigrants. The changing of laws alone created a postcolonial environment but did not lead to a greater unity among different people groups, settlers, and natives. In the new South Africa, descendants of British settlers as well as Afrikaners and White Europeans are supposed to have somehow become natives, and their status as immigrants unites them in their solidarity with Black tribal counterparts, who continue to be categorized and separated under customary law.

The accumulated wealth of White South Africans continues to benefit that same group economically, without long-lasting efforts toward redistribution of wealth; and the economic disparities and chasm of wealth along racial lines continues to grow. Efforts to merely eliminate the racist laws without redressing the consequences of economic, educational, and social injustices as a result of decades under these laws, are incomplete at best—and at worst, they are a mockery of repairing systemic injustices.

The influence of foreign invaders may have caused irreparable damage to the nations in southern Africa. British presence on the higher education system is apparent, but it is more challenging to distinguish because of the prominent Dutch Afrikaner rule. However, the history of higher education in the wider context of the continent of Africa continues to be relevant to a discussion of how the postsecondary system in South Africa has evolved. While the majority of African universities are national, public institutions, there is still no Pan-African classification system to replace the colonized education model that remains in place. The impact of the apartheid system in South Africa for nearly fifty years cannot be underestimated, but it is merely the fruit and not the root of White dominant, anti-Black ideology and policy from European invaders across the southern African region over hundreds of years. According activists, students, and professors we spoke with, the root of resistance is in the conscientization of Black South Africans. The image of Steve Biko was on the shirts of many students and the philosophy of liberation shaped their discourse. As we toured Robben Island, the solitary incarceration of Robert Sobukwe stood as a monument to the revolutionary Pan-Africanist movement. He was a professor that was considered so dangerous that he could have no contact with anyone. Black knowledges and liberation are a threat to White supremacy and are a root of the decolonial future.

5
Shades of Advantage in Brazil

> Latin America is the region of open veins. Everything, from the discovery until our times, has always been transmuted into European—or later United States—capital, and as such has accumulated in distant centers of power.[1]
> —Eduardo Galeano

The Indigenous peoples of South America (e.g., the Tikuna, Tupinambá, Tapuia, Arawak, Carib, Aimoré, Gaurani, and Ge) were hunters, gatherers, fishers, and farmers. They cultivated a wide variety of crops and developed preservation techniques to store harvests underground, which allowed civilization to flourish. The richness of the lands with a canopy of trees for miles on end, the life-giving rivers flowing, and an abundance of wildlife—like colorful toucans, hummingbirds, parrots, monkeys, jaguars, pumas, and anteaters among others—created a beautiful tapestry of life in the lands of what is now known as Brazil. The peoples of these lands spoke hundreds of distinct languages and dialects. The Indigenous peoples lived in harmony with nature, taking only what was necessary.

The Tikuna people emerged in a region that overlapped Brazil, Colombia, and Peru. In their origin story, one of the cultural figureheads, Yo'i, fished people out of the waters of the Eware:

Yo'i, tired of being alone and wanting to populate the earth and make the world more joyful and complete, caught the fish from the river, one by one. But only animals came with the hook, always male and female together: this is how the animals came into being. But Tetchi arü Ngu'i wanted the husband, and Yo'i wanted human beings: how to catch them? He decided to replace the bait with manioc: thus, everything he caught began to transform into beings similar to him, humans, who ran around on the land. This is how humanity came about, and this is how the Magüta people came about.[2]

Through the retelling of this story and the customs that went along with it, the Tikuna people addressed questions about their origin and survived with a sense of purpose regarding their existence. Knowing where they emerged from helped to set a course for where they were going.

European Contact and an Invasion of Brazil

After establishing a trade route from West Africa to Portugal in the late fifteenth century, bringing enslaved Africans to Portugal, the Portuguese fed their appetite for conquest by funding enterprises disguised as altruistic explorations. In April of 1500, Pedro Alvarez Cabral led a Portuguese expedition departing from west Africa and heading west, which led to the naming and claiming of Brazil for the Portuguese crown. Initially, Brazil was set up merely as a trading port, not intended to be settled—but in order to protect their resources, the Portuguese militarized and weaponized their colony to defend their trade monopoly. Through subjugation and integration, religious conversion, and spreading of diseases, the Portuguese took control over the coastal regions of Brazil from the Indigenous population.

The introduction of the slave economy produced an entirely unique White diaspora, even after slavery laws were abolished. With a history of miscegenation among the Portuguese, Indigenous, and enslaved Africans, a durable Brazilian national identity was formed, cloaked in a White diasporic substructure. This chapter examines the case of the only Portuguese-speaking country in the Americas, through the lens of the "Tools of Invasion" referenced in chapter 2, to unpack the distinctive ways the Portuguese established an enduring legacy of their invasion of Brazil through religion, empire, an appetite for conquest, science, and capitalism/economy. How were the Portuguese able to invade Brazil without the need for legions of troops, frigates, destroyers, or warships, and how did this invasion imprint the White diaspora into the fabric of Brazilian society?

Beginning in 1500, Portuguese invaders made their first contact with the Brazilian coast. Initially, the Brazilian operation was merely used as a resupply and trade port. The native population traded natural resources, namely the brazilwood, for shiny objects like knives and European novelties objects.[3] The

FIGURE 13 Museum docent describing the Candomblé wood carving in the Afro-Brazilian Museum run by the Federal University of Bahia (UFBA). (Photo by author.)

brazilwood and other resources soon caught the attention of other invaders, including the Dutch. This newfound competition for control over the resources of Brazil instigated colonization. The Portuguese sent a number of expeditions to ensure the monopolization and elimination of the competition for Brazilian resources. By some historical interpretations, the Portuguese were able to successfully colonize Brazil in part because of their willingness to integrate with the native population through relationships and culture.[4] As the Portuguese invaders' roots in Brazil became fortified, the importation of approximately four to five million enslaved Africans reshaped the Brazilian landscape.[5] A vast majority of enslaved Africans were sent to Brazil.

During the period of slavery in Brazil, the introduction of enslaved Africans further fractured the conception of race in Brazil. Some among the Indigenous population, especially those who intermixed through marriages and conversion to Catholicism, were afforded status in Brazilian society.[6] With an estimated 170 million Catholics, Brazil today has the highest number of Catholics in the world, which emphasizes the importance of Catholic conversion during this span of history. One main reason for the predominance of Catholicism is the infusion of African and Indigenous religions through Candomblé, which evolved in Brazil through a practice of syncretism. As described to us by our museum guide, Candomblé is a religion with a supreme God and many other

FIGURE 14 Artwork from the Museu Historico Nacional in Rio de Janeiro depicting the rural plantation lifestyle in Brazil. (Photo by author.)

minor deities. The idea of praying to a minor deity is similar to the Catholic practice of praying to a patron saint. All have their own deity to guide their destiny and protect them. The Candomblé ritual includes a song and dance where worshipers become possessed by their deities.

As the Portuguese further exported their culture, the plantation lifestyle became glamorized. Buaroque de Holanda eloquently captures this mimicry by stating:

> One of the effects of improvising, nearly by force, a kind of urban bourgeoisie in Brazil was that certain attitudes, which up to that time were peculiar to the rural patriarchate, soon became commonly adopted as the ideal norms of conduct for all classes. The manor-house mentality, stereotyped through long years of rural life, thus invaded the cities and conquered all occupations, even the humblest. John Luccock of Rio de Janeiro witnessed a typical case: a simple carpenter dressed like a nobleman, with a tricorn hat and buckled shoes, refused to use his own hands to carry his tools, preferring to have a black man handle them.[7]

Other historical accounts document the ways in which manual labor was "socially scorned as something just for blacks" and was perceived to be performed only by those who were inferior to White people.[8] Figure 14 is a

FIGURE 15 *Monument to the Bandieras* in São Paulo. (Photo by author.)

photograph of artwork we saw during our visit to the National Historical Museum in Rio de Janeiro: it depicts a White man being carried in a hammock by two Black men, with two Black boys carrying additional accessories, including an umbrella and the White man's shoes. This artwork captures the rural lifestyle with a sense of mockery, as if even walking is too laborious for this White man.

In the São Paulo region of Brazil, the White dominant ideology was so pervasive that the Portuguese invaders began "bandeira" (flag) expeditions to push settlement inland and westward, to enslave the Indigenous population, claim territory under the Portuguese flag, and search for precious resources like gold and diamonds. These "bandeirantes" consisted of very few White Portuguese with a majority of the expedition comprised of enslaved Indigenous and mamelucos (European and Indigenous mixed). The bandeiras repressed and subjugated the Indigenous population beyond the more coastal Portuguese colony. As seen in figure 15, these bandeiras are canonized with a larger-than-life *Monument to the Bandeiras*. We had a chance to view this memorial to the Portuguese invasion at the entrance to the prominent Ibirapuera Park in São Paulo. The launching point of many of these bandeiras was the present-day São Paulo region of Brazil. A large number of the Indigenous people captured by the bandeiras were enslaved to work in Paulista society in wheat farming production, to aid in the war with the Dutch in northeastern Brazil.[9]

Brazil successfully repelled the Dutch in 1654, cementing the Portuguese claim of Brazil for the crown.

Concurrent with and paradoxical to notions of White dominance, there was also miscegenation among Africans (i.e., Blacks or *pretos*), Indigenous people, and Whites. "There was a special nomenclature for racial mixtures: people were known as mulattos; mamelucos, or mixtures of Indian and white; curibocas or caboclos, near whites or descendants of white men; and cafusos, or mixtures of Indians and blacks."[10] Given the prevalence and longstanding cultural acceptance of racial miscegenation, the resulting social hierarchy was based less on rigid concepts of binary racial classifications; instead, it was a hierarchy based on skin color and adjacency to Whiteness.[11] This hierarchy is similar to the classification system developed in South Africa and discussed in chapter 4. There is no question that race has been a constant source of political and social discourse in Brazil, heightened further by the ending of slavery in Brazil in 1888 as systems of Whiteness and power structures grasped for control.[12] In one such policy decision to maintain White dominance, the Brazilian government "subsidize[d] and prioritize[d] European immigration from the 1880s to 1920s."[13] This Whitening of Brazil displaced Afro-Brazilians from both land and labor. Johnson and Heringer state, "The government often gave Brazilian-born whites, as well as new primarily European immigrants, employment, housing, education, and other financial opportunities and advantages."[14] The education system, including the universities, was one of the arms utilized in the maintenance of White dominance. This further exacerbated the arduous prospects for Afro-Brazilian advancement.

In 1792, the first symbols of a higher education institution in colonial Brazil were founded in the Polytechnic School (the Escola Politecnica), followed by the National College of Medicine (Faculdade Nacional de Medicina) in 1808. The University of Rio de Janeiro (Universidade do Rio de Janeiro) unified the assortment of colleges that were established in the greater metropolitan area. In 1937, the University of Rio de Janerio became the University of Brazil (Universidade do Brasil); and in 1965, while under a military dictatorship, it became the Federal University of Rio de Janeiro (Universidade Federal Rio de Janeiro) (UFRJ), which has remained the name of the institution. As the crown jewel of the federally funded university system in Brazil, UFRJ has been a focal point for political power and racial conflict, eventually giving rise to education reformation. The Brazilian national identity and the conceptualization of race in the broader social context have had considerable influence on the role of universities in Brazil in maintaining White dominant systems.

The rise of eugenics in England and the United States in the 1880s shaped ideas of justifying racist ideologies and validating them through science (pseudoscience). The eugenics movement made its way to Brazil through the pseudoscientific writings of Raimundo Nina Rodrigues, who studied at the Faculty of Medicine in Bahia, which is now affiliated with the Federal University of Bahia.[15] Rodrigues, one of the first anti-Black scholars in Brazil, wrote on the inferiority of Black and Indigenous people, which he claims led to the degeneration of Brazilian society. Under the banners of anthropology, law, and medicine, and with the validation of a university education, Rodrigues propagated racist ideologies through newspaper articles, books, and scholarly journal articles.

The São Paulo Eugenics Society was established on January 25, 1918. "Its founding represented the first step in the organized history of eugenics in Latin America and the beginning of a more or less continuous involvement by Latin Americans in eugenics from 1918 to 1940s."[16] The president of the society was Arnaldo Vieira de Carvalho, who helped found the medical school in São Paulo. Like Rodrigues and Carvalho sought to explain and remedy social problems with science and public health policy.

> The São Paulo Eugenics Society had an initial success, holding regular meetings in the hall of the Santa Casa de misericordia, the traditional meeting place of the state's most important scientific group, the Medical and Surgical Society. From the beginning the society defined itself as a learned, scientific, professional organization from which would flow scientific studies, conferences, and propaganda on the physical and moral strengthening of the Brazilian race. In fact, the society, despite its distinguished roster of medical scientists—most of them clinicians—carried out no research. Its main function was to propagandize the idea of eugenics and to introduce a new language into Brazilian debate. Traditional medical themes—alcoholism, venereal diseases, degeneration, fertility, natality, tuberculosis were linked to the "purification" and eugenization of the nation.[17]

The São Paulo Eugenics Society exported its pseudoscientific eugenics movement to other Latin American countries, including Mexico, Peru, and Argentina. Furthermore, the eugenics movement in Brazil validated public policy debates enshrining notions of heredity, race, and gender through anti-immigration laws, racism, segregation, sterilization, and other racist policies under the guise of sanitation and public health.

When the main building of the University of São Paulo's medical school opened in 1931, a bronze bust of its founder, Arnaldo Vieira de Carvalho, was placed in front of the building, recognizing the founding of the medical school by the former São Paulo Eugenics Society president. The lasting legacy of racism and hatred is still enshrined at this site today. In 2020, the institution recently celebrated the one-hundred-year anniversary of Arnaldo Vieira de

FIGURE 16 Bronze bust of Arnaldo Vieira de Carvalho in front of the University of São Paulo School of Medicine. Photo from Wikimedia Commons website.

Carvalho's death.[18] The immortalization of Carvalho has provided an unending legacy of White supremacy indoctrinated at the universities in Brazil. There is no question that Carvalho and the São Paulo Eugenics Society played a vital role in spreading racism and anti-Blackness throughout Central and South America. Yet the historical record has been sanitized to revere him as a great man in Brazilian society.

Persisting Challenges in Brazil

Schwartzman and Paiva concluded that "Brazil's long history of colonization and slavery has resulted in a country where race and socioeconomic disadvantage are strongly correlated."[19] Racial classification plays an important and persisting role in White dominance. Students who grow up in lower-income areas like the Brazilian City of God neighborhood have limited access to high-quality elementary and high school education.[20] Conversely, citizens growing up with high socioeconomic backgrounds have families who are able to afford high-quality schooling for their children.

In Brazil, the more prestigious universities are the publicly funded and tuition-free institutions like the University of São Paulo and UFRJ. White and light-skinned high-income families are able to send their children to the more prestigious universities, which are free. Meanwhile, lower-income students, who are often Black or dark-skinned people of color, receive free elementary and secondary education and are tracked into lower-status private universities that charge premium tuition. In 2001, the Brazilian government adopted affirmative action policies. The implementation has created considerable tension in Brazilian social and political discourses, as some believed that importing this foreign ideology would have a negative impact on Brazilian society because of the perceived differences in the conception of race in Brazil as compared to the United States.[21] The affirmative action policy created new questions about what it means to be Black in Brazil, given the country's long history of miscegenation. With an influx of White applicants claiming Afro-Brazilian ancestry, so-called "verification commissions" were formed, effectively serving as racial tribunals, to confirm an individual's self-reported racial identity based on gross generalizations of phenotypes.[22] The White diaspora created a society with clear and unquestionable status and advantages for White Brazilians and those with White adjacency. In this instance, not being White on paper allows White Brazilians to continue to dominate the social, economic, and educational structures even when policies were designed to recompense Afro-Brazilians and other disenfranchised communities of color.

During our travels to South America, we spoke with scholars about the verification commissions. They explained that a committee would make observations of the candidates' phenotypical traits, including things like nose width, hair texture, skin pigmentation, fullness of lips, and, most interestingly, nail cuticles. The commission believed that people of African ancestry have a dark pigmentation in the tissue around their fingernail cuticle, as opposed to those with European- only ancestry, who will have a pinker pigmentation around their nail cuticle. This racial determination panel's procedure brought back a century-old approach to racial pseudoscience. This form of racial classification was challenged by a test case of fraternal twins, one of whom looked Afro-Brazilian with a darker skin complexion, and the other of whom could pass for White.

Conversely, in places where there are fewer White people (e.g., Salvador in the state of Bahia), the lighter Blacks are able to occupy the positions that White people would occupy in more White regions (e.g., São Paulo). Sociologist Reginald Daniel observes that "multiracial individuals in Brazil have historically sought to maximize whatever social rewards accompany their partial European ancestry, typically refraining from speaking out on questions of racial inequality."[23] This long history of silence dates back to the times of enslavement, when light-skinned Afro-Brazilians were concerned about social changes disrupting their status in society.

During our travels to Rio de Janeiro, we were able to visit the Santa Marta favela, which is an informal settlement on the mountainside of the city. As seen in figures 17 and 18, the Santa Marta favela has breathtaking views overlooking the city, with a spectacular panoramic of Sugar Loaf Mountain and the *Christ the Redeemer* statue. Our guide, a resident of Santa Marta, told us some of the history of that particular favela. After the abolition of slavery in Brazil,

FIGURE 17 Photo of Santa Marta favela in Rio de Janeiro, Brazil, painted in bright colors on the side facing the city in a beautification effort. (Photo by author.)

FIGURE 18 Panoramic view from the Santa Marta favela with a view of the city, Sugar Loaf Mountain, and *Christ the Redeemer* statue. (Photo by author.)

many of the freed Afro-Brazilians were chased out of town by White Brazilians. The Afro-Brazilians fled and hid in the uninhabited hillside. They would make their way down the hill daily to find work in the urban centers. The anti-Black political ideology ushered in by the Brazilian eugenics groups and others led the way to the founding of favelas like Santa Marta, Santa Teresa, City of God, and Rocinha, among others.

One of the most famous literary works of Brazil is *Child of the Dark*. In this book, Afro-Brazilian Carolina Maria de Jesus chronicles her life with her children in a favela in São Paulo. In her diary, she recounts her efforts to provide for her family by searching the favelas for things to recycle, like paper and tin cans. In describing the impact of a favela on its residents, Carolina Maria de Jesus wrote in her diary on May 20, 1958: "Sometimes families move into the favela with children. In the beginning they are educated, friendly. Days later they use foul language, are mean and quarrelsome. They are diamonds turned to lead. They are transformed from objects that were in the living room to objects banished to the garbage dump."[24] This diary entry paints a vivid picture of a dissolute environment with limited social mobility for favela residents. A capitalistic economic structure often creates disparities of haves and have-nots. However, the overlay of anti-Blackness and White supremacy ideology concentrates the burden on Afro-Brazilians, who are trying to provide for their families. Lower-income residents of Brazil, who tend to be in high proportion Afro-Brazilians, are forced to live in these conditions due to a White dominant economic structure that exploits labor from Black bodies but does not promote social mobility.

The favelas and other urban areas where Afro-Brazilians reside are rife with anti-Black sentiment as it relates to public policy, closely resembling a colonial structure, particularly regarding the distribution of power. Sociologist Jaime Amparo Alves uncovers stories of the state of terror in which Afro-Brazilians find themselves in São Paulo, which is notorious for spatial and residential segregation and the mass incarceration of Afro-Brazilians. Alves states:

> In urban Brazil, rampant killings by the police through counterinsurgency and warlike tactics may well affirm the status of black "criminals" not just as lawbreakers but also as foreign enemies of the state. As the weeklong police slaughter of alleged "criminals" in the streets of São Paulo in May 2006 demonstrates, the state responds with terror rather than violence when confronted with the black body. Even when the state responds with incarceration, black prisoners do not stop being enemies of the state as they are not just mere menaces to public safety but also permanent threats to the core values of Brazilian society. That is why the black movement has been vocal in denouncing killings by the police as "targeted assassinations" and mass incarcerations as "political arrests" to highlight the ideological underpinnings of policing practices in Brazil. Within the Brazilians' racialized regime of law, the black enemy is subjected to the states' decisive power through police terror or permanent confinement in zones of nonbeing.[25]

Our tour guide in the Santa Marta favela spoke of similar issues through a process he called "pacification," in which the police came into the favela and arrested or killed all those suspected of being criminals. This "pacification" in Rio appears to mirror the tactics used by the São Paulo police. As we walked past a few places within Santa Marta, our guide pointed out a barrage of bullet holes in the sides of various structures. Given the vast economic disparities, observable anti-Black sentiment, and the overt and covert forms of White supremacy embedded within political ideologies, opportunities for Afro-Brazilian social mobility are apparently and severely limited.

Afro-Brazilian Social Movements

Legal slavery ended in 1888 in Brazil with no subsequent era of legal segregation (which is distinct from the 1865 ending of slavery followed by one hundred years of Jim Crow in the United States). White supremacy and anti-Blackness existed under a veil of racial democracy, which included the promotion of European immigration, the rejection of African immigration, and the promotion of miscegenation. Brazil had similar goals to those of South Africa and Australia in its effort to eradicate and control the Black population and maintain a society rooted in White supremacy, although its approaches differed. While South Africa and Australia opted for overt oppression and violence, Brazil's brand of oppression and violence took place in the disguise of racial harmony.

The notion of Brazil as a great racial democracy is prevalent in the mythos of the world's perception of the country. As Twine observed in a study of Afro-Brazilians and Euro-Brazilians from a range of socioeconomic statuses: "The Afro-Brazilians argue that since they are not formally prohibited by law from entering an institution, racism is not the reason for their exclusion from universities and higher education. The absence of state-sanctioned barriers to access to education is emphasized; informal, de facto forms of exclusion are rarely considered."[26] Brazil's strong sense of national identity is founded on the premise of Gilberto Freyre's version of a racial democracy.[27] In this view of Brazilian society, socioeconomic status rather than race is usually blamed for inequality. During our discussion with Brazilian scholars, one professor noted, "If you see a school with all Afro-Brazilians, you would say the school is for lower-class students, not Black students, because Brazilians talk more about class than race." This was a common theme that we heard as we discussed some of the pressing challenges of Brazilian society. Socioeconomic status was often the topic of our conversations, and not racism or systematic oppression. The ideology of racial democracy often paints a utopian image of Brazilian society that erases the horrors of the invasion and conquest of Brazil by the Portuguese. Herringer and Johnson note, "Critics of racial democracy have argued that the celebration of racial mixture, or miscegenation, has left elements of the earlier ideologies of whitening and white supremacy intact. Positive connotations of whiteness and negative connotations of blackness remained strong in Brazilian national identity, society, and culture."[28] Afro-Brazilians are not immune to the barrage of images of the racial utopia that Brazil projected around the world. The first order of the Black social movement in Brazil was to convince Afro-Brazilians that their limited social mobility is due to racism and systemic oppression and not due to class. Additionally, the Black social movement in Brazil has to thwart off accusations that its perspectives are anti-Brazilian.

Starting in 1978, the Movemento Negro Unificado, or Unified Black Movement, fought for the teaching of Afro-Brazilian history and culture and to reveal racial inequities and oppression. This movement made significant strides; in 1998, the Brazilian Ministry of Education, with the consultation of Afro-Brazilian leaders, adopted the National Curricular Parameters, which acknowledged the need to better support the diversity found within Brazil:

> The diversified portion of the curriculum should express the contents incorporated by the educational systems as well as the priorities set as part of the school project and reflect the students' inclusion in their curriculum development. It must take into account the possibilities of a basic preparation for work and a deeper concentration on a given course or field of knowledge, in the form of courses, projects or modules in line with the interests of the students or those in the community to which they belong. It is important to make it plain that the development of the diversified portion of the curriculum does not mean professional training but rather a diversification of school experiences with the purpose of enriching the curriculum or even further concentrating studies on a given field of knowledge, when and where the context so requires. The main objective is to develop and consolidate field-specific knowledge, in a contextualized fashion, by linking knowledge to social and production practice.[29]

This component of the National Curricular Parameters makes an attempt to provide a culturally relevant curriculum that might further engage all Brazilian students in making connections with their education and community.

Another important event within the Black social movement was the state visit of Nelson Mandela in August of 1991. At the time, Mandela had been recently released from his political imprisonment under the apartheid regime in South Africa. In his first remarks to an audience of Brazilian government officials and those who were likely to provide assistance against apartheid, he stated that Brazil as "a successful multiracial society would serve as a 'guide' for South Africans."[30] Mandela went on to say that "black Brazilians had already reached the stage where they could use their own resources, leaders, and schools for their betterment," juxtaposing them with Black South Africans, who were striving for voting rights.[31]

The Afro-Brazilian activists were less than enthusiastic about these remarks and publicly noted that Brazil, like South Africa, was led by a White ruling class that represented only a minority of the country's population. One difference that the Afro-Brazilian activists noted was the openness with which Whites in South Africa expressed their racism. Additionally, they observed that the economic struggles of Afro-Brazilians were similar to those of Blacks in

South Africa.[32] After meeting with more Afro-Brazilians during his visit, Mandela later doubled back on his previous comments while in Salvador (in the predominantly Black Brazilian state of Bahia) by stating, "We are confident that the Brazilian people will courageously confront the problem of racism in Brazil, as the American people were able to do in the 1960s."[33] Mandela's observation emphasizes the ongoing struggle for justice in Brazil, a reversal of his earlier comments acknowledging Brazil as a racial democracy. The narrative of Brazil as a racial paradise has been an image projected around the world; and Mandela, like many others, had naively bought this conceptualization wholesale.

During our visit to Brazil, we met with the Black student group Coletivo Negro Carolina de Jesus at the Federal University in Rio de Janeiro. They still held many grievances regarding issues facing Afro-Brazilian students, such as the lack of integration of Afro-Brazilian contributions into the university curriculum. We observed other student protests that conveyed their concerns by displaying photographs of various dorm rooms, which are not furnished by the university. Some photos depicted the rooms of White and high-income students, who had palatial residences with loft beds, refrigerators, microwaves, desks, chairs, and adequate lighting. Other rooms were occupied by lower-income students, who were often Afro-Brazilian or a mixture that included African heritage. Unfortunately, these rooms did not carry the same amenities as those of their higher-income White counterparts. The photographs depicted rooms furnished with only a sleeping bag, a milk crate for a desk, and a desk lamp. Moreover, we observed that at the dining services that offered subsidized meals for students, equivalent at the time to $1.75 (in U.S. currency), the line was filled primarily with students of color. We asked several students how long it might take to get their food, and they replied that "it can take over an hour, but I have to wait because I cannot afford the other choices." On the other hand, with myriad unsubsidized dining options available in the neighborhood surrounding the university, White students had little problem finding nourishment between classes.

These disparities demonstrate the persisting impact of a political ideology that favors White supremacy and anti-Blackness. Similar to what Fanon identified about colonization, "the cause is effect: you are rich because you are white, you are white because you are rich."[34] The canons and machines described by Fanon are intricately woven into the highly stratified economic society in Brazil. The canon in Brazil has become the racial democracy and colorblind ideology emphasizing a strong national identity over all other social identities. The machines in Brazil are the various ways White supremacy and anti-Blackness pervade the capitalistic economic structure. The canon and the machine create an environment where White Brazilians maintain socioeconomic dominance.

Decolonizing Brazil

The fight to decolonize Brazil starts with the recognition of the lasting impact that colonization has had in embedding notions of White supremacy and anti-Blackness within all facets of Brazilian society. The fallacy of a racial democracy must come to an end. When we were in Brazil, it was apparent that White supremacy permeates all aspects of Brazilian life. For example, there are settled notions of beauty in Brazilian culture, as demonstrated by all the major fashion magazine covers featuring phenotypically European models and very few, if any, covers featuring Afro-Brazilians. There are also clear labor hierarchies for different types of employment: Afro-Brazilians were the cooks and janitors (at the back of the restaurant) while White Brazilians were the cashiers and servers (at the front of the restaurant). Geography and race are often interconnected, and in this case, the residential racial segregation in major metropolitan areas like Rio de Janeiro and São Paulo were vivid and disconcerting.

A decolonizing of the land and the curriculums will include a recognition of the many contributions made by Afro-Brazilians and Indigenous populations to Brazilian society. This includes but is not limited to seeing representation within the curriculums of both historical figures and current artists, scientists, athletes, and authors. The only way to achieve true social mobility in Brazilian society lies in having representation in all aspects of social, civic, and political life. Decolonizing the environment in which Brazilians are raised and educated will require a shift in formal institutions like universities, which play a key role as keepers of culture while operating a number of museums in Brazil that depict how people groups and culture are perceived. Moreover, universities train primary and secondary teachers—are they equipped to teach with culturally responsive practices that challenge and support all students?

Lastly, decolonization must shed light on Indigenous populations who have endured despite the White invasion. Brazil is often discussed in a Black, White, and Mixed triad, with the Indigenous population often left out of the discussion. In an ongoing struggle, the Indigenous peoples in the interior of Brazil fight to protect their lands within the Amazon and in other more rural regions of Brazil. Current Brazilian President Jair Bolsonaro's policies seek to rescind the demarcation of Indigenous land for the purposes of further economic development and land exploitation.[35]

In this chapter, we shed light on the root and fruit of anti-Black ideology and systemic racism in what some refer to as the liberal democracy of Brazil. Despite the fact that more than half of all Brazilian citizens identify as Black, and having the distinction of having the largest population of Black African descent outside the continent of Africa, Brazilian anti-Blackness continues consciously and unconsciously in this nation. It has been reproduced via generational, educational, societal, and political means. In 2018, President Jair Bolsonaro made reference to Black citizens as cattle, and critiqued them for failing to even procreate. This was not the first time anti-Black comments were uttered by prominent politicians. Two years later, Vice President Hamilton Mourão declared that there was no more racism in Brazil. His comments came in the aftermath of a protest over the death of João Freitas, an unarmed Black Brazilian man, in the city of Porto Alegre. Black Brazilians continue to suffer from overt anti-Blackness, colorism, and other forms of racial injustice.

However, there may be opportunity for change on the horizon. Black Brazilians have recreated *quilombos* to fight the ongoing injustices. A quilombo is a rural community created by Black Africans who escaped enslavement generations before slavery was finally abolished in 1888. Roughly three thousand quilombos are still in existence today. In the spirit of unity and solidarity, young Black Brazilians are creating new urban spaces to honor Black heritage and liberation. These new urban quilombo spaces exist as forms of resistance to anti-Blackness, systemic racism, and colorism. Afro-Brazilians in these communities have the ability to self-govern. Quilombos provide an opportunity for restoration with a return to African cultural norms like a more collectivist orientation. These communities are also removed from the horrors of police brutality and murder confronted in large urban centers like São Paulo and Rio de Janeiro.

There is no question that a truly decolonized Brazil will take an ongoing and painstaking effort toward progress. In South Africa, the Cecil Rhodes statue fell at the public University of Cape Town. Rhodes falling was symbolic of a growing social movement rejecting White supremacy. Similarly, in Brazil there are tangible symbols of White supremacy, like the bust of Arnaldo Vieira de Carvalho located at the public University of São Paulo School of Medicine. Arnaldo Vieira de Carvalho was a racist and president of the São Paulo Eugenics Society. Like Rhodes, Carvalho, too, must fall.

6
Empty Treaties and Occupied Land in Oceania

> Oceania is vast, Oceania is expanding, Oceania is hospitable and generous, Oceania is humanity rising from the depths of brine and regions of fire deeper still, Oceania is us. We are the sea, we are the ocean, we must wake up to this ancient truth and together use it to overturn all hegemonic views that aim ultimately to confine us again, physically and psychologically, in the tiny spaces which we have resisted accepting as our sole appointed place, and from which we have recently liberated ourselves. We must not allow anyone to belittle us again, and take away our freedom.[1]
> —Epeli Hau'ofa

The spiritual force or power throughout many of the cultures of Oceania is known as *mana*. The ocean is a vast ecosystem that embodies both peril and reward in proximity to mana. The double-hulled canoes used to traverse extensive stretches of the ocean in between islands are filled with mana. The people, cultures, and knowledges that took cues from the stars, the wind, and the ocean to be the earliest and most skilled navigators in human history embody mana. Humans lived on the land mass now called Australia up to forty thousand years ago, and peoples like the Lapita travelled between islands throughout Oceania for the last three thousand years.[2] Use of natural resources, languages, and fragments of pottery are all insights into a distant past of a type of ingenuity and integration with the world that is still present in peoples and knowledges today. From Hawai'i to Aotearoa and from Tahiti to Australia, the cultures of Oceania are scattered throughout the largest body of water in the world and a ring of fire that can generate a new island on a whim—and they are all connected by mana.

Aotearoa was not the first land mass to be settled in Oceania, but it bears witness to the great cultures, knowledges, and mana of Oceania. The creation story of the Māori is laid out in three major cycles: the sky, the earth, and, broadly, the symbiotic relationship between nature and humankind. The personification of nature in the Māori narrative is a foundational indicator of the holistic worldview. Humans were created as "belonging to the land: as tangata whenua, people of the land."[3] In this way, they are not above the rest of nature but are interdependent and within nature. This origin dictates a meaningful and ongoing relationship characterized by reverence. People living in Samoa and Tonga, in the millenniums preceding their arrival in Aotearoa, used their natural surroundings to develop an incredible ability to navigate the vast ocean using the stars while sailing in their double-hulled canoes made from the trunks of trees. The ability to traverse thousands of miles of ocean preceded Columbus by seven centuries. The establishment of language, tribes, family units, integration with nature, hunting, navigating, and the maintenance of society through deep belief systems is a rich history of knowledge production and diffusion that was threatened by settler colonialism, but that persists throughout Oceania today.

The simultaneous destruction by colonial invasion and persistence of Indigenous peoples sets the context of this chapter. The small canoe pictured in figure 19 is a motif of the ingenuity reflected among the wayfaring groups around Oceania. A canoe this size is used for a small distance, but the design mirrors the larger size used for longer journeys to other islands. The robust existence of knowledges and practices is a witness to the ancient and contemporary cultures of the many groups of island peoples—much of which is not accounted for in the modern university canon. The primary focus of this chapter is Australia and Aotearoa/New Zealand, but we also include our experiences in Vanuatu and Hawai'i as context for the broader knowledge expansion driven by the mana in Oceania. We also detail key moments of invasion from Europe, the development of the university, and in the final section, hope for the decolonized future.

FIGURE 19 Canoe in Vanuatu, South Pacific. (Photo by author.)

European Contact and Invasion

The sailor/explorer/invader James Cook was commissioned to map the Pacific Ocean in 1768. The name "Pacific" was given to the large body of water by another sailor two centuries earlier, Ferdinand Magellan, who ironically found the body of water to be pleasant and calm upon entry, and gave it the name peaceful—Pacific. Magellan was killed by people in the Philippines in 1521 after converting thousands to Christianity. His final efforts resulted in a battle in which his life was ended by a bamboo spear. Cook was the first European to make contact with people in eastern Australia and Hawaiʻi and to circumnavigate New Zealand. When he first saw people on the coast of Australia, he made a note that they were a dark or black color, giving an early indication of the racialized and anti-Black influence of the European mental and colonial lens applied to peoples in first contact. On a later voyage, he was sailing in Hawaiʻi and in need of resources and boat repair. Stealing wood, as well as disagreements between Cook's men and the Hawaiians, led to a conflict that ultimately resulted in his death on the shores of Hawaiʻi.

Dumont D'Urville, in his nineteenth-century voyages throughout the Pacific Ocean, developed the demarcations of Polynesia (many islands), Micronesia (small islands), and Melanesia (black islands). The descriptions of Polynesia and Melanesia included phenotypic characteristics of race and connected to a mentality that was linked to stages of civilization and development. For

Polynesia D'Urville described people with long brown hair and light brown skin, followed by reflections on their strong work ethic and creativity. For Melanesia, descriptions of black skin and wooly hair were followed by reflections of a slower work ethic and a lack of intention. He literally mapped anti-Blackness onto the cultures of Oceania with a parallel hierarchy of savagery and skin tone. These divisions later became "scientific categories" used in textbooks persisting into our contemporary geographic understanding.[4] The people of New Caledonia and Vanuatu were grouped into Melanesia and were observed by "naturalists" who connected the physical differences related to skin tone as belonging to a different species. These were early clues as to how the concepts of Black and White were not binary, but rather hierarchical social constructs on an intersectional spectrum that included geography, culture, belief systems, and gender roles. Anything noted as a "discovery" about peoples and cultures was essentially an imposition of a European lens. This invasion took place not just physically, but also culturally and epistemologically.

The First Fleet of ships that embarked from Europe to Botany Bay, Australia, stopped at known ports in Brazil and South Africa, which are at the core of this study in terms of the location and diffusion of settler colonialism and White supremacy. In those locations, the fleet of ships brought onboard plants and animals that European colonizers thought might be valuable in their new settlement in Botany Bay. As we tracked the knowledge diffusion from Europe through settlements that became White diasporas in the Global South, the route, activities, and dispositions of this fleet are significant. In Australia, the land was deemed *terra nullius*—meaning that even though people were already there, the land was considered wasted because the people there were not perceived to be engaging in the use or cultivation of the land. As a result, the nonfarming Aboriginal people were not offered a treaty, as they were not seen as landowners.[5] This was different from Aotearoa, where the Māori were overtaken through a series of complicated exchanges and treaties (e.g., the contested Treaty of Waitangi of 1840 between the British and Māori). Australia and New Zealand emerged as the two White majority powers in this region. The national identity went from settler colonial to White nationalist through power that decimated the Aboriginal and Māori populations. The fruits of these invasions are visible by varying degrees but are deeply connected to the roots of conquest supported by the function of the university in knowledge production, diffusion, and the confirmation of credentials.

Australia

Invasion

The first British fleet arrived with the intention of settling Australia in 1788 and stunned the Eora people living there. With a thousand people unloading equipment and animals from the ships, "the invaders behaved like savages, landing without permission, and then felled trees, and cleared the ground of undergrowth and pitched shelters."[6] The Aboriginal Eora observed the settlers for two years before much contact occurred. The British had negotiated treaties with other Indigenous peoples, but following Captain Cook's observation that the land was "waste" and essentially unowned, the designation terra nullius gave way to the prevailing view that there was no ownership there and that the British would be the first settlement with rights to the land. All of the tools of invasion were used to grow the notion of civilization. Christian missionaries founded churches, unfamiliar laws were established to govern land and behavior, trade for food and tools was the beginning of economy, and scientific records developed to understand how Australia might successfully be settled. During the first few decades of settlement, violent conflicts, the spread of disease, and the stress on natural resources drastically reduced the Aboriginal population.

Medical and scientific visions cultivated what it meant to be White in the 1800s and early 1900s, as a settlement was reconfigured into a nation by White peoples who found a way to adapt to a new and initially uncomfortable climate.[7] The social constructs of Whiteness that later evolved leveraged the authority of European pseudoscience and included body type, head circumference, response to disease, and gender constructions of virility and femininity. The construction of Whiteness as a racial category in Australia was a social signal pointing to the "essence of Whiteness."[8] Some of the most poignant forces establishing White dominance were medical science and public health, which "came to provide a rich vocabulary for social citizenship in an anxious nation" as "doctors counseled politicians and the public on how to implant and cultivate a white race across the continent."[9] University-trained medical doctors became resident experts on how the White person could adapt to a new territory, which makes the medical construction of a White-dominant Australia a story of immigration, politics, eugenics, adaptation, nationalism, citizenship, and medicine.

A key movement in the formulation of Whiteness in Oceania was identifying the medical and adaptive problems of White people in a new region of the world away from the homeland. For example, was it the humidity, climate, and sunlight that caused people to struggle, suggesting an environmental issue, or was it something else? Dr. T. P. MacDonald, an Australian and university-trained physician, made the argument that it was actually tropical disease as opposed to tropical climate that was the true enemy of the White race.[10] This important distinction would later help to make the argument that non-White peoples in Australia were the problem (i.e., the disease carriers), as opposed to the climate. In an address to other scientists about the topic, MacDonald surprised the conference audience by singing:

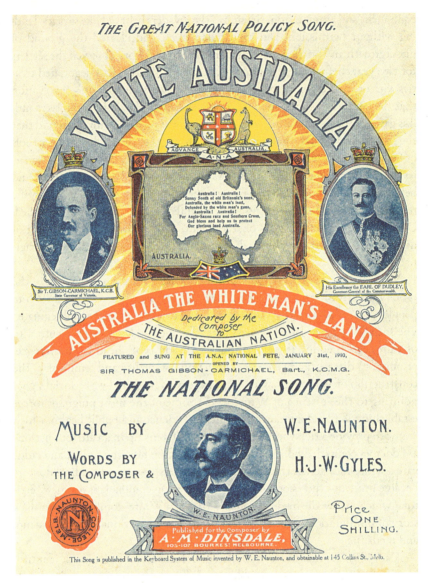

FIGURE 20 Sheet music for "White Australia," 1910, Museums Victoria.

Hail her, White Australia, hail her!
In the warm Pacific sea,
Rising from the mists that veil her;
Beautiful is she.[11]

Figure 20 is an advertisement for the sheet music to the national song "White Australia." In the dialogue between the White homeland (Britain) and the newest White diaspora (Australia), physicians commented on the inferiority of White people bred in tropical climates as opposed to those bred at home. These pseudoscientific discussions were the seeds of defining Whiteness somewhere between the center of Europe and the "uncivilized" peoples of the "undeveloped" Global South.

By 1912, a notable essayist wrote that citizens "believe in racial purity" and that the word "Australia" is built on the idea of a biological White superiority.[12] In addition to the construction of Whiteness, medicine also provided a rhetoric for "talking about territory and a means for taking imaginative possession of it" and later a logic for "social citizenship and a means for living up to it."[13] Racial science was a foundation for the architecture of colonization and the establishment of White dominance that led to White nationalism in a place like Australia. If the entire medical and social establishment in the White-dominant country is rooted in a knowledge system based on creating homogeneity, uniformity, and racial purity, then how might that influence a contemporary understanding of Whiteness? The manifestations of Whiteness that continued on the continent included the removal of Indigenous children from their families and a history of racial violence.[14] The knowledge and logic systems at the root of this type of violence are connected to the education system in Europe that was transplanted around the world.

Higher Education

The first university in Australia was the University of Sydney, founded in 1850 by William Wentworth and Charles Nicholson. Wentworth was born on a ship and was the son of a convicted prisoner and an aristocratic landowner. He was sent to England for an education and returned to Australia to join the government. Nicholson was born in England and earned the degree of medical doctor and at the request of an uncle became a doctor on a ship headed to Australia in 1834. He served in government positions and participated in the founding of the university before becoming chancellor in 1854.

In the earliest documents that recount the inspiration for founding a university, some commentators in the new settlement lamented that it had taken too long to establish a university that could confer a degree since the British had arrived.[15] The lament was justified by pointing out that it took less than twenty years after the founding of New England to establish Harvard, while in Australia they had no place to send their "sons" except the "distance of half the globe" back to England.[16] The University of Sydney was established on land that was taken from the Gadigal, the original owners and first peoples of the land. Only eighteen months after the invasion of 1788, the land was being repurposed for education, religion, and personal estates.

Wentworth's contributions to the founding of the university have persisted in the historical spotlight. Some of his earliest comments about the university were related to religious tolerance and openness—indicating that no religion shall be barred from entrance. The nod to religious tolerance, however, did not shape his point of view about the Indigenous peoples of the land. After participating in land acquisitions that amounted to attempted genocide, he referred to Aboriginals as "orangutans" and "wild men." In his 1819 book, he wrote: "The aborigines of this country occupy the lowest place in the gradatory scale of the human species," and provided several examples of how his Darwinian perspective supported his racist claim, including references to physical features resembling people from Africa with skin the color of "a dark chocolate" and dispositions that are "rude and barbarous."[17] Like many universities around the world, the University of Sydney has a central building named for the founder and an accompanying statue on the campus (pictured in figure 21).

We observed the statue in the Great Hall at the center of the campus during a graduation ceremony. Wentworth's statue was towering over the graduates. The statue and the Great Hall are located in a larger area at the center of the campus known as the Quadrangle. At an entrance to a large courtyard, we noticed a schematic of Cambridge University with an explanation of how the architecture at the University of Sydney is designed to mimic Cambridge and Oxford. The transplanting of architecture is a symbol for the logic, methods, and curriculum that were established to the exclusion of Aboriginal knowledge, people, and culture. It was not until 1963 that the first Aboriginal students were even admitted to the university.

As we walked around the university attending various lectures and interviewing faculty staff, and students, we found no visible presence of Aboriginal culture other than a land acknowledgement in a low monument on the lawn on the side of a building. The university claimed a broad focus on multiculturalism and diversity, including what was described by one professor as the category of "CALD, which means culturally and linguistically diverse, but I think it also means that someone from France fits in the category." The student newspaper highlighted some cultural tensions on campus, and the archives in the library gave some history of the growing diversity of the institution. As we sat in the graduation ceremony and observed admissions tours of the campus, the vast majority of the names we heard called out (above 90 percent) were of East Asian origin. The overarching impression we got of the student body was that it was largely White and Asian. Just off of the campus there were mostly Japanese ramen and Chinese noodle restaurants, and Mandarin was spoken frequently. The Gadigal Centre, which is advertised as providing support for Aboriginal and Torres Strait Island students, looked very much like all of the other buildings on campus, with tables, chairs, computers, books, and a few pieces of art on the wall. This was in contrast to what we observed in Aotearoa/New Zealand, where signs were in Māori language,

FIGURE 21 Statue of Wentworth in the Great Hall at the University of Sydney. (Photo by author.)

and art, architecture, history, and imagery of all kinds were visible around the universities we visited.

In March 2019, during the course of our study, a massacre took place in Christchurch, New Zealand. An Australian man entered a mosque and committed a mass shooting, murdering and injuring dozens of Muslims. The tragedy awakened people everywhere to the ongoing threat of racialized violence. In response to the massacre, the vice chancellor of the University of Sydney quoted Wentworth in an email about the terrorist attack:

> Dear students,
> Following my message in Monday's *Student News* regarding the recent terrorist attack in Christchurch, I would like to again extend my deepest sympathies to all those effected. Yesterday I met with SUMSA (Sydney University Muslim Students' Association) representatives to offer support and to reinforce our commitment to ensuring that the university is a place of inclusion where people from all cultures, religions and backgrounds are welcomed, respected and valued.
>
> The University's founder, William Charles Wentworth, told the Parliament of NSW in 1850 that the University of Sydney needed to be a place "whose gates are open to 'the disciples of Moses, of Jesus, of Mohammed, of Vishnu, of the Buddha." His vision of a diverse University is one to which we remain strongly committed.

The email was regarded by people we spoke with as misguided and offensive. Quoting someone who was racist against Indigenous peoples does not enhance the credibility of the university's founder, despite his notions about religious diversity and openness. Only months later, students began a Wentworth Must Fall movement that in some ways reflected the Rhodes Must Fall movement of South Africa. Shortly thereafter began a smaller counter campaign titled Wentworth Must Stand, which supported the study of Western civilization and denounced accusations of White supremacy.[18]

Universities are largely Western institutions that operate on White logic with a history of White dominance. The University of Sydney is no exception. There are paradoxes here, as well: in addition to a past checkered with White supremacy and contemporary debates on how founders and large donors are honored/treated, there are also degrees, faculties, and centers dedicated to acknowledging and exploring the past while being committed to a better future. One author described an initiative of the University of Sydney in the following way: "Aboriginal and Torres Strait Islander participation and engagement is a core component of our future and an essential part of our collective history. Five years ago, we launched *Wingara Mura-Bunga Barrabugu* ('thinking path to make tomorrow'), our Aboriginal and Torres Strait Islander higher education strategy. The strategy aims to expand Aboriginal participation in education and research, and indeed our own cultural understanding. *Wingara Mura-Bunga Barrabugu* is a commitment to work together to respect and empower Aboriginal and Torres Strait Islander cultures and perspectives as an integral part of our University."[19] It is difficult to accomplish this type of initiative while maintaining statues and buildings of Wentworth at the epicenter of campus with White and Western ideas still at the center of the curriculum, but that is the complexity of a university.

Another contemporary debate we encountered during our time on campus was about The Ramsay Centre for Western Civilisation. This center operates at the University of Sydney, but it also faces opposition due to its focus on White, European influence. According to the center's website, it was created because the founder and others "believe generations of young Australians will eventually... learn to value their own civilisational heritage."[20] Some members of the University of Sydney community pointed us to a movement of resistance against The Ramsay Centre, which they described as a "far-right initiative to prevent broader engagement with anything that isn't White, European, or in pursuit of international students who pay a lot of tuition." This coincides with reports of a majority Aboriginal staff at universities experiencing racism and discrimination.[21] At only 3 percent of the Australian population, Aborigines represent a disproportionate number of the incarcerated, underinsured, underemployed, and undereducated. The combination of attempts to preserve and present White/Western heritage as the center of knowledge is intertwined with anti-Blackness and Indigenous oppression. The roots of how it happened in the past provide insight for how and why it has mutated into the form it exists in today. That Wentworth still stands verifies the imprint and image of White supremacy. Framing the removal of Wentworth and other monuments as historical erasure obscures the fact that it is in fact a historical recovery. The violence enacted by colonial settlers installed the conditions for White supremacy and erased bodies and knowledges and then miseducated the masses with a monocultural and Eurocentric logic and curriculum. Removing the monuments is connected to decolonizing the imprint and the ideology.

This brief and selective recounting of the history of invasion/settlement of Australia, the formation of racial identity and White supremacy, and contemporary notions of violence and contest all serve to demonstrate the roots and fruits approach we take to understanding social systems and institutions. Often the contemporary issues around race and Indigeneity are viewed in an isolated and decontextualized manner, which separates the fruits from the roots. The fruits are byproducts and have to be situated with the sources of the issues, which are connected to misguided notions of pseudoscience around race and the violent concepts of civilization used to justify the powerful appetite for conquest. In our observations and interviews, the notion of connecting racial identity with White supremacy as a root was largely strained. This came across as ironic, from our perspective, given the explicit nature of the White Australia policy. The universities in Australia have pockets of resistance and conscientization, but these were not as visible as those on the neighboring island.

Aotearoa/New Zealand

Invasion

Tāmaki is a stretch of land in Aotearoa settled by several different Māori tribes. It was fertile and therefore good for farming, and it was eventually "purchased" in 1840 by a colonizing official by the name of William Hobson, who named the territory Auckland (after a benefactor by the same name). This took place in the same year as the Treaty of Waitangi, which was signed by Māori chiefs and British settlers. It marked the beginning of a British claim of sovereignty over "New Zealand." Over the next twenty years, Tāmaki and other regions of Aotearoa were settled by colonizers seeking resources and wealth.

Prior to that critical event, Dutch explorer Abel Tasman had the first European encounter with the Māori in 1642, and Cook made three voyages to New Zealand in the 1770s. Decades after Cook's visit to Whitianga, a chief recounted an encounter with a European ship for the first time when he was a child. He described the boats, paddles, and activity of the Europeans buying Māori articles. He recounted, "When that first ship came to Whitianga I was afraid of the goblins in her, and would not go near the ship till some of our warriors had been on board. It was long before I was reconciled to those goblins or lost my fear of them. At last I went on board of that ship with some of my boy-companions, where the supreme leader of that ship talked to us boys, and patted our heads with his hand."[22] The interactions were not always so friendly. Early encounters resulted in the loss of life; and even as communication became more fluid over time, it revealed some of the deeper perceptions among the groups of people. One of the Māori recounted a disagreement that was settled and in reflection added, "We did not invite you to our shores for the purpose of plunder and murder; but you came, and ill used us: you broke into our tabooed grounds. And did not Atua give those bad white men into the hands of our faithers?"[23] This critical reflection on miscommunication was an early indication of the events that would take place next. The first organized group of settler colonizers was in 1814 from the Christian Missionary Society. These settlers had a difficult time convincing the Māori of their religion, and outright disagreement about the creation story demonstrated the confidence the Māori held in their belief system. Some Māori told missionaries their creation story might be true for Pākehā (term for White settlers), but they understood Aotearoa to be fished from the sea, as told by their ancestors. In the early years, some Pākehā came to believe the same as the Māori, and any Māori that accepted Christianity tended to syncretize the two belief systems.[24]

The designation of terra nullius was not given to Aotearoa, so the British could not occupy and claim ownership. A group of private investors called the New Zealand Company and their commitment to colonial land acquisition, combined with missionary speculation about regulation and unrest, fueled a rationale for British intervention. In February 1840, the Treaty of Waitangi was drafted in English and translated for the Māori signatories. With assurances of land and protection, the treaty had five hundred signatures by September 1840. The translation, the meaning of the treaty, the process (which excluded Māori input or revision), and the aftermath all reveal problems within the treaty, which is still discussed today. Only three years after the treaty was signed, armed conflicts began over land disputes. One Māori leader called the document a "rat trap" and said that "if the Pākehā want our country, he will have to fight for it, for we will die upon our lands."[25]

Notions of cultural superiority and racial supremacy clouded the interactions between Pākehā settlers and the Māori. Increased numbers of settlers also created increased demand for work by the New Zealand Company, which was working more hastily to acquire profitable land. By 1860 a series of wars began as a byproduct of a treaty without parity.

Higher Education

Like other educational efforts from colonizers to Indigenous peoples, early educational ordinances dictated that instruction be distant from their homes in order to rapidly assimilate the students out of the influences of their villages. Instruction was in English even though under the 1867 Native Schools Act, there was an attempt to maintain some cultural practice. By 1905 teachers were using corporal punishment for students who did not speak in English and the entire system demanded cultural surrender in language and identity.[26] The University of Otago was established in 1869 as the first institution of higher learning, with support and financial backing from the Presbyterian Church, which also funded a chair in mental and moral philosophy. In 1870 the University of New Zealand was established by colonial officials, including the Oxford-educated John Andrew Chapman, who was raised in England by banking and clergy families and arrived in New Zealand in 1856. By 1880 the origins of the University of Auckland (UA) were in place, but the university existed as an official branch of the University of New Zealand beginning in 1893. A couple of years later, the neighboring Auckland University of Technology (AUT) was established.

With English- and Scottish-educated officials at the helm, universities in New Zealand existed as reproductions of leaders' alma maters. Through decades of land wars and colonial practices that disenfranchised the Indigenous peoples, some universities have gone through extensive programs and policies to make these institutions more in tune with Māori knowledges. In addition to Māori centers of learning, academic disciplines and journals, student programs, and architecture, all of the signs we saw at both UA and AUT were written in both English and Māori. There is a Māori-centered university about a four-hour drive from Auckland called Te Whare Wānanga o Awanuiārangi, which explores and integrates Māori ways of knowing as the central learning style. The presence of Māori language, architecture, and imagery at these universities creates a unique paradox and tension in institutions constructed on Western ideas and principles.

In our interviews, we gleaned some hesitancy to talk about race. One participant mentioned that ethnicity is used in the census and the term Pākehā is used casually, but he went on to ask the question, "How White is White? How Brown is Māori?" In spite of hesitancy to talk about race, this professor observed that "deprivation, disease, and wealth runs along racial lines." Another professor of social science encouraged us to go to the place where the Treaty of Waitangi was signed and to take note of how "indigeneity is presented as overt or visible, but it is still marginalized"—a critique he also made about universities in New Zealand. Another professor said, "We are in combat mode at the university—our Indigenous colleagues are miserable." The Pākehā and Māori tensions were clear in the interviews and were also woven into what one scholar called a "global anti-Blackness which exists all over the world and is very prevalent in Auckland."

In the contemporary environment of universities, there has been an increase in White supremacist activity—primarily among students. Students told news outlets that since 2013 pride movements related to European heritage and a "Dominion Movement" have become visible on campuses.[27] An open letter was republished in a news outlet and targeted the University of Auckland. One excerpt from the letter was about understanding the Treaty of Waitangi and its principles (often summarized as partnership, participation, and protection):

> The University of Auckland has an online course that is mandatory for all students to teach them the principles of academic conduct and integrity. A mandatory course of this nature should be implemented in regards to Te Tiriti o Waitangi. The University of Auckland's "Strategic Plan 2013–2020" emphasizes the University's commitment to Te Tiriti, stating in Objective 11 that one of its key actions is to "develop and implement strategies to assist all staff and students to have a knowledge and understanding of The Treaty of Waitangi/Te Tiriti o Waitangi relevant to their disciplines." Making a course like this mandatory would be an important step towards this goal.[28]

Another excerpt focused on European and Western perspectives in the curriculum: "In many of our classes, we are taught content that centres European perspectives and histories, at the expense of all other forms of knowledge. This alienates non-Pākehā students and robs us of educational opportunities. We implore the academic disciplines at the University of Auckland to incorporate more non-Western ideas, theories and scholars to their curricula. Centering

Western perspectives normalises Western ways of thinking as the only legitimate forms of knowledge. This offers fertile ground in which white supremacy can flourish."[29] A few months later, in October 2019, more White supremacist activity emerged on campus, and staff and administrators published an open letter denouncing the movement and encouraging the university to take actions.[30] Reports of racial harassment are increasing, and a fear-driven climate reflects an increase in White supremacist activities on campuses around the world. The anti-Black, settler colonial, Eurocentric ways of understanding the world are the roots and context that created the conditions for universities to not only play host to these viewpoints, but also to cultivate and incubate them.

Decolonial Future

The people we spoke to who worked with Māori-centered learning had the most resolute and radical approach to education. This comes as no surprise, because they center the knowledges of the people and culture that have been there the longest. One scholar we interviewed described a critique of settler colonialism as the "great White exchange," explaining, "Settlers arrived and transferred physical diseases because of their presence and wrecked physical and social health of the Indigenous peoples. Two hundred years of deprivation and diseases in Indigenous communities are still present. Now it is not just because of a physical presence alone, but also an ideological and economic White dominance, which is a new form of colonialism."

In speaking about efforts to encourage the expansion of Māori thought and support Māori students, the scholar continued: "We do not see our role as indigenizing the institution. The university has an international focus which devalues the local and Indigenous. We have a mutually exploitative relationship: resources in exchange for university association with Māori excellence. Instead of race, there are conversations about unconscious bias, which is a conversation. It allows a lot of conversation and people to go, 'Whoops' and to take no responsibility. We lack robust conversations of race." These sentiments were part of a visible and palpable sense of critical consciousness at the University of Auckland. Figure 22 depicts a sign that was posted on a bulletin board. The issue addressed in the text of the sign relates to fishing rights and a campaign to vote against a bill that does not recognize the fishing rights of the Māori. The title of the sign also evokes the history of treaties dating back to the contested Treaty of Waitangi in 1840. The rhetorical question implies that a deal is never settled when the government is involved. As a Māori administrator at another university commented, "The law in the eyes of many of the poor is an ass—because of the people who created the laws." The consciousness of the problems with treaties was very present. It was akin to the way Queen Liliuokalani's

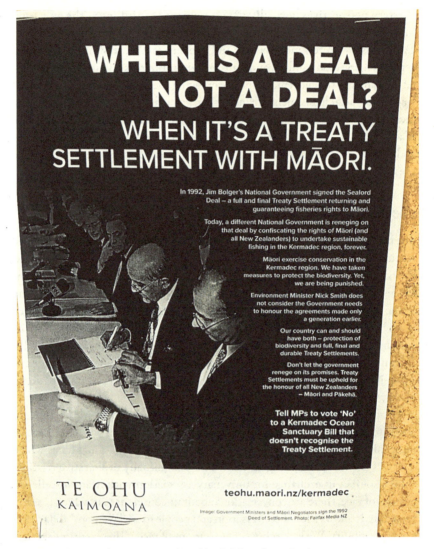

FIGURE 22 Poster at the University of Auckland. (Photo by author.)

letter to the United States president protesting the illegal overthrow of the Hawaiian Kingdom in 1893 is still present in the consciousness of Hawaiian students and scholars.

The state of settler colonialism turned White supremacy and anti-Blackness seems undefeatable at times. It leads us to ask the question, what is the future and the future for decolonizing the university? A Māori scholar asked a similar question during an interview: "How does Māori knowledge inform and lead?" It is a profound question, and the scholar/administrator continued to say, "Combining Māori knowledge and practice and improving the mobility of Indigenous students is our objective. Britain's history still says we were 'discovered by Cook in 1769.' Telling Indigenous stories by Indigenous people is important, or else children grow up to believe lies [and] that they are criminals. Māori ontology must always be included in Māori epistemology. Together they represent an opposing philosophy to that of dominating the Earth. Instead, it is about working together with the Earth." The profound words and ideas resonated in similar ways with many of the people we interviewed and in the visible signals we observed on multiple campuses.

In the book *A Third University Is Possible*, la paperson succinctly creates a challenge to the reader in thinking about different types and purposes of the university. The third university is one of decolonizing resistance and is named as such in relationship to the third world. La paperson admits to resisting, giving clear descriptions of what this university might look like in order to avoid either utopias or appropriation, but writes: "Te Whare Wānanga o Awanuiārangi in Aotearoa might be the clearest example of a decolonizing university in formation."[31] The history of the university begins with Māori cosmology to situate their ontology and then presents the struggle for identity brought about by the colonial invasion of missionaries, whalers, and settlers. In spite of the struggle that has been part of its history, the university affirms, "We define our own future," and in its story is written, "Today, we still evolve as a unique indigenous institution. We deliver education that makes a difference in the lives of our students by accepting them and enabling them to take pride in their cultural associations."[32] Te Whare Wānanga o Awanuiārangi's vision of itself is rooted in the land, ancestry, ontology, cosmology, and epistemology of the Māori. It is not bound by the conventions of White and Western European ideologies and practices. In this way, the past is also the present and the future, and it is a profound antidote to the cultivation of White supremacy and anti-Blackness, precisely because the university is working from a different and distinct root system.

Conclusion

Decolonized Past and Future

> Yet colonial schools carry decolonial riders...
>
> My position is impossible, a colonialist-by-product of empire, with decolonizing desires...
>
> I desire against the assemblage that made me.[1]
>
> —la paperson

During a research visit to Australia, at the end of an interview, a thoughtful scholar pulled a small book off of a nearby shelf. While thumbing through the pages, he said, "I feel like you are trying to name something that is unnamed, or has yet to be named." He opened the Chinese classic text *Tao Te Ching* to the first chapter and read:

> The way that can be described is not the eternal Way.
> The name that can be spoken is not the eternal Name.
> The nameless is the boundary of Heaven and Earth.
> The named is the mother of creation.
>
> Freed from desire, you can see the hidden mystery.
> By having desire, you can only see what is visibly real.

> Yet mystery and reality emerge from the same source.
> This source is called darkness.
> Darkness born from darkness.
> The beginning of all understanding.[2]

That particular moment sat with us throughout the many phases of this project. Similarly, Roland Barthes approached the namelessness that Lao Tzu referred to as exnomination.[3] Barthes coined this phrase to convey a phenomenon in which the bourgeoisie could hide their name, and by extension, their identity. By not referencing themselves they were able to maintain an undetected hegemonic power of ideology, culture, routine, and practices. To be unnamed can protect the grotesque and insidious nature of systemic violence.

In reality, much of what we are writing about has been named, and we have been diligent to select and cite the most poignant thoughts on the concepts we are trying to describe. In other ways, the shadows, ghosts, and connections between concepts have been more difficult to grasp. Part of that is because notions of superiority are shifty—and White supremacy is a ghost that appears and reappears in a perpetual haunting. It is rooted in anti-Blackness, colorism, and settler colonialism. In order to preserve the image, imprint, and ideology of Whiteness, it had to have a symbolic opposite in a category of Black. In this way, the notion of Black is essential to White existence. This came to fruition in many ways, including through colonizing invasions and the Enlightenment. Toni Morrison once remarked in a lecture, "One purpose of scientific racism is to identify an outsider in order to define one's self."[4] In the origin of the other we find the pursuit of self-definition intertwined with supremacy.

On the cover of the book is an image and an event that guided this project—when student action resulted in Rhodes falling at the University of Cape Town. The movement in Cape Town reverberated back to the White homeland (England) where the Rhodes Must Fall movement picked up steam at Oxford University. It also connected with other White diasporas wrestling with colonization in the move for Wentworth to fall in Sydney. Perhaps in the near future there will be more calls for Carvalho to fall in São Paolo. Yet the tenacious connection between settler colonialism and White supremacy yields a colonial irony. Though Rhodes fell at UCT, another Rhodes monument sits on the hill above the campus. We also took note of a student in 2021 connected to the National Society of Black Physicists who was named a Rhodes scholar. In a press release the award was noted as the oldest and most prestigious scholarship program enabling people to study at Oxford. The irony highlights that it is not just the image of the monument, but the roots of the monument in the form of imprint and the ideology that enable a White supremacist logic to persist through miseducation and historical erasure.

The pedestal beneath the statue on the front cover represents the root system that undergirded not only the construction of the monument but the entire existence of the campus and curriculum. The tools of invasion are not only roots, but also the fibers that intertwine to form a multipurpose rope, which we excavated in chapter 2. Audre Lorde's poem *For Each of You* implores people to examine things they hate before discarding them.[5] La paperson goes further to say that "understanding technologies provides us some pathways for decolonizing work."[6] From our roots and fruits perspective, the contemporary fruits cannot be understood without the contextualization of the roots. Our process of excavation was to examine the core of the rope—the appetite for conquest. La paperson also highlighted this approach: "We can identify projects of collaboration on decolonial technologies. Colonizing mechanisms are evolving into new forms, and they might be subverted toward decolonizing operations."[7] Excavation of these realities does not stop at mere understanding. The image on the cover also demonstrates that the rope that makes up the tools of invasion might be subverted to pull down the statues and firmly rooted figureheads of coloniality, racism, anti-Blackness, and persistent epistemological violence.

Having presented historical reviews of colonization as well as examples of practices that have emerged as a result of White diaspora via three distinct case studies, we pause to reflect on how root systems of the past continue to bear fruit in the present. The contemporary fruits of supremacy are sometimes hidden and sometimes visible and violent in all three regions today. In one particularly horrific example mentioned in chapter 6, on March 28, 2019, a 28-year-old White Australian man committed a massacre at two mosques in Christchurch, New Zealand. Many people were injured and fifty people died. The shooter claimed allegiance to White identity, and he even inscribed his guns with the names of crusaders against Muslims. The writings of the perpetrator reveal the imprint of an ideology undergirding his violent actions: White entitlement has been part of the very structure of Australian society and White nationalism.[8] With reference to the White Australia policy of a century ago, the same types of sentiments emerge today with violent tendencies.

A year prior to this massacre, Australia was considering providing fast track visas for White farmers to leave South Africa under "horrific circumstances," including land seizures and violence.[9] Australian media had previously reported that considerations of new land policies by South African President Cyril Ramaphosa were connected to the murders of White farmers on a regular basis. This led to Australian officials welcoming White farmers to a more "civilized" country like Australia. The vast majority of private farmland in South Africa is owned by White farmers, and since the end of apartheid rule, up to half a million White South Africans have left their country, with Australia as the most popular relocation destination.[10] When Nelson Mandela visited Brazil in

1991 following his release from a long political imprisonment, he initially thought it was an example of how South Africa should evolve racially. Only a short time later did he recognize the fruits of a global White supremacy that was also firmly rooted in Brazil. Though these events might easily be viewed as disconnected, they demonstrate an ongoing type of colonial connection across White diasporas nested in the Global South. Furthermore, they have a history and a context, and the disputes over the land that was at the core appetite for conquest are still being present.

Meanwhile in South Africa, where some publicly celebrate the formal abolishment of apartheid policies and highlight the economic success of certain Black citizens, much of the fruit of White supremacy has mutated into various forms of silent resistance that have been difficult for some to recognize and name. A vast majority of Black South Africans continue to live without basic necessities in townships scattered across the country—a consequence of generational accumulation of wealth during, as well as long before, apartheid policies took root. Some public displays of resistance like the #RhodesMustFall campaigns continue to shed light upon ongoing efforts to decolonize. Yet many current and former Black South African students continue to suffer silently as the mechanisms of a half century of racist policies remain deeply rooted within economic, educational, and societal systems for the majority of Black or "Coloured" citizens.

In Brazil, the public persona of post-racial achievements due to the multicontextualized culture of Blackness creates a false sense of achievement regarding the issue of anti-Blackness. Anti-Blackness in Brazil manifested in a racialized hierarchy that created class systems, and classifications were determined simply and crudely by physical measurements of hair type, skin color, nose width, and other constructs. The same was true in apartheid era South Africa. In both cases, the results had a catastrophic impact on those who were downgraded; the levels of inequity in healthcare, education, employment, and general quality of life were manifold and long-lasting.

Within tertiary education systems in all three regions, a similar phenomenon can be observed. That is, the perception of quality and academic rigor of a given higher education system in any of these regions may be determined by how many light-skinned or White students are enrolled at these universities.

In an examination of coloniality, we build on the perspective that the precolonial has a unique connection with the postcolonial. It is not a linear existence or process, and neither is the movement toward decolonization, which is, "put bluntly, the rematriation of land, the regeneration of relations, and the forwarding of Indigenous and Black and queer futures—a process that requires countering what power seems to be up to."[11] As scholars and administrators become drawn to the movement to decolonize, there will be calls to define and demarcate what constitutes decolonization. There will be important questions along the lines of understanding when decolonization might be happening.[12] These are important and practical discussions that may help to avoid some confusion, appropriation, or use of buzz words to signal an intent without a real vision or means.

The colonizing tools of invasion represent a shifting and effective collection of strategies. The university as a social institution plays a role in all of these, particularly as it relates to preservation. Regarding the history of academic subject areas or disciplines, their emergence is rooted in a technology or method of preservation. The academic or scientific perspective, or gaze, then becomes authoritative in a knowledge hierarchy and can unwittingly make a contribution toward an ongoing colonizing type of violence. Eugenics was a movement and a powerful combining of the tools of invasion, which injected into academic disciplines the root of a dangerous pseudoscience. Figure 23 shows the academic subject areas as the roots of eugenics, defined as the self-direction of human evolution. The caption below the image says, "Like a tree eugenics draws its materials from many sources and organizes them into a harmonious entity."[13]

A racialized, anti-Black, White supremacist view of the world not only shaped by eugenics but also the greenhouses that incubated and preserved the movement—universities.

Under the settler colonial and Enlightenment-driven demarcations of knowledge, the ecology of knowledges is lost to binaries such as prehistory versus history, formal versus informal, and myth versus fact. Then, in an effort to define and preserve, comes a close relative of knowledge hierarchies: destruction.

To preserve can also serve to destroy. The double edge of codifying knowledge is to preserve it for future generations to view—but such preservation also disrupts an ecosystem based on interdependence with nature. James Cook was offered a double-hulled canoe as a gift, and if it had fit in his ship and had been taken back to Europe, it might have been preserved for generations to come; but since it was not, most of what we do know about the people who made it is preserved only in narratives that have been passed through the generations.

The academic disciplines that make up universities are deeply implicated in this world. The roots of the eugenics tree are still in operation. One of the best examples of the roots and fruits issue is the use of methods that are often treated as neutral. Statistics is often described as a method to describe and interpret the world, but the history of how it was developed and applied—and how it continues to be misapplied today—fits squarely within the phenomenon of the colonizing university.[14] Overfamiliarity with methods as a signal for truth has produced generations of unquestioned assumptions. Each academic discipline, each canon of knowledge, each accepted method can be excavated for the ways in which it preserves and perpetuates the same anti-Blackness and sense of superiority that its development was rooted in.

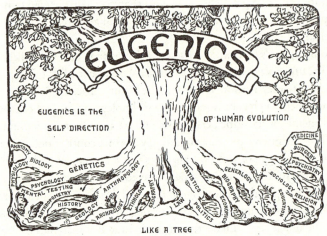

FIGURE 23 A Eugenics Congress 1921, in Harry H. Laughlin, *The Second International Exhibition of Eugenics*, American Museum of Natural History, New York.

The White normativity of the Global North shapes the White architecture and corresponding logic systems across Europe and North America. Normativity shapes dominance to the degree that Whiteness operates like a translucent ghost—it has a powerful impact but is hard to see. Universities play a key role in both reinforcing dominance through the academic canon and in other cases dismantling dominance through deconstructionist frameworks like antiracism and decolonization. This makes a study of Whiteness in the Global South a compelling way to inspire a move away from the decontextualized and uncritical acceptance of academic truth.

White dominant societies in the Southern Hemisphere have existed as a White diaspora with unique conceptions of superiority. The connections across the Southern Hemisphere have been established since the origins of the colonies. Historical and contemporary events share a lineage and a root system in the diffusion of the White centrality of Europe. Universities play a key historical role in both constructing and disseminating knowledge. As arbiters, controllers, and constructors of knowledge in all disciplines, higher education institutions become important sites to explore as they relate to the social construct of race and identity. The degree to which White logic has manifested in the White diaspora through universities is the degree to which there is resistance to diverse ways of knowing and anticolonial curriculums. Furthermore, race was intricately connected to knowledge, and ideas developed under the umbrellas of science and religion, creating an unholy alliance with a protective covering from the "community of scholars" housed at institutes of higher learning.

The laws governing colonies and the architecture of the institutions were set forth in supremacist blueprints, and the roots of it all sit unexcavated below the surface. Even still, we find hope and inspiration for a decolonial future. Propositions upon which a decolonizing university can be built are proposed by la paperson. To find a third university and a decolonizing approach, la paperson imagines the following:

1. It already exists. It is assembling. It assembles within the first and second universities.
2. Its mission is decolonization.
3. It is strategic. Its possibilities are made in the first world university.
4. It is timely, and yet its usefulness constantly expires.
5. It is vocational, in the way of the first world university.
6. It is unromantic. And it is not worthy of your romance.
7. It is problematic. In all likelihood, it charges fees and grants degrees.
8. It is not the fourth world.
9. It is anti-utopian. Its pedagogical practices may be disciplining and disciplinary. A third world university is less interested in decolonizing the university as a decolonizing university.
10. It is a machine that produces machines. It assembles students into scyborgs. It assembles decolonizing machines out of scrap parts from the colonial technology. It makes itself out of assemblages of the first and second world universities. To the degree that it accomplishes these assemblages, it is effective.[15]

We saw glimpses of all of these propositions in the regions and institutions we visited. We also saw a massive resistance to the movement to decolonize. There is a persistence in allowing anti-Blackness to come to the surface in the name of quality. There is a tenacity to describe Indigenous knowledges as myth or informal. Social justice requires cognitive justice, and the ecology of knowledges will be required for the survival of knowledges. The land and the bodies sustained by the land carry knowledge and understanding that goes well beyond the Western academic canon. The communities that know and live interdependently with the land, and the small corners of universities that reflect these understandings are our teachers. They embody ancestors, narratives, and knowledges that take us beyond the trajectory of global White supremacy. They bring us to places where we are both quiet and also craving Indigenous wisdoms, Black ingenuity, and a deep connection to the land. We crave these like water to nourish roots that are both old and new, the past and the future.

Whiteness and anti-Blackness both remain as powerful ideologies in Australia, New Zealand, South Africa, and Brazil. Power and privilege planted deep into colonial root systems have evolved into manifold tools of invasion. The roots bear fruit that complexifies the ongoing effort toward decolonization and indigenization of curriculums and culture. Even when White citizens are in the minority, it does not negate the ubiquity of White power, privilege, and supremacy in these spaces. Moreover, even as Whiteness is contested and challenged in various academic areas, Whiteness is simultaneously reified and centered in the academy. Moreover, in the context of non-White majorities, the indigenization of the state, and efforts toward economic reparation, White power and privilege suppress most liberation movements and postcolonial campaigns.

White supremacy and the culture of Whiteness continue to influence the ideologies on both the colonizer and colonized minds. Theologian and philosopher Willie Jennings, whom we referenced earlier in this book, defines Whiteness as "a way of perceiving the world and organizing and ordering the world by the perception of one's distorted place within it. But it is also more than a perception: Whiteness includes the power to place that perception on other people and to sustain it."[16]

Upon further examination of the three case studies, we underscore the pattern and predictable cycles of invasion, and the overlaps are intriguing. During the early part of the fifteenth century, in the era of conquest, the Portuguese, Dutch, French, and British were in a race toward territorial expansion, to name and claim new territories in a rapidly emerging campaign of exploitation. The unquenchable thirst for possession was initially quenched by the discovery of land, which was named and claimed for king and country. Indigenous people already present and existing within their societies were then subdued and enslaved, and proselytized, either in obedience to misguided theology or in service to the goal of expansion. The discovery of natural resources—and in two of the three regions, the discovery of gold and diamonds—ushered in a new order of invasive practices. Trading companies created ports and weigh stations upon previously inhabited lands. Militarization and commerce went hand in hand with religion and education. The common ideological undercurrents in all three regions were as follows: Native and Indigenous people were exploited, enslaved, proselytized, educated, and civilized. Universities were established for several key reasons: first, to educate the colonizers to become erudite and learned citizens; second, to prepare a workforce to maintain and improve the mining of precious stones; third and finally, the university existed to level the playing field for lower-class settler colonials to compete with the upper-class elites back home.

The final analysis on colonization is that supremacy evolves and mutates. As we have demonstrated in the chapters of this book, White dominance and anti-Blackness have gone hand in hand as part of the roots of colonization. Even as land treaties are overturned and racist laws such as apartheid in South Africa and the White Australia Policy in Australia have been removed, White dominance has not been eradicated in the mind of either the colonizer or the colonized. Minds continue to be named, claimed, and colonized, even if the lands and properties cannot. This then, is the key function of the university and the greatest threat to a liberalized, free-thinking, conscientized citizenry.

Acknowledgments

Acknowledgments take many forms. We first and foremost recognize the many people who have helped bring this research project and book to fruition. Our first acknowledgment is a recognition of the students who acted out of a responsibility to their communities and out of a deep awareness of who they are: student-activists who risked everything, and some sacrificing their lives for the cause of justice. The cover of the book is reminiscent of a moment and a movement that was born out of the consciousness and initiative of students in the Rhodes Must Fall and Fees Must Fall movements in South Africa. We acknowledge that similar efforts by students have occurred in other places like Australia, New Zealand, and Brazil. To see their work and influence in action was both inspiring and revealing about the work around the world still to be done in the wake of White supremacy.

We express our gratefulness to all of the colleagues who spoke with us, both informally and formally, to reveal their values, their experiences, and their ways of understanding the world both in and around the university setting. Some of the wisest and most generous people we have ever spoken with contributed to this book, and we are forever indebted to them. One in particular is our colleague Dr. Vuyelwa Jacobs. During our visits to South Africa over the course of five years, she spent a great deal of time making pathways to help us contemplate, grow, understand, and experience the places she calls home. Dr. Jacobs is a one-of-a-kind scholar and friend. Dr. John Volmink similarly offered his time and expertise in ways that exhibited a great deal of gravitas. He is someone who has been persistently gracious and challenging through our years of knowing him. Dr. Jenny Lee is a global scholar whom we also have the honor to call friend. She has been kind enough to offer direction and feedback throughout this project. Her scholarship continues to inspire us. We are grateful for everything these folks, and many others, have contributed to bring us to this point.

Another type of acknowledgment that we have engaged in throughout this project is our own positions of dominance in concert with our constant search for a sense of justice. We confess that this book has been an important part of our development—with the caveat that our growth is ongoing and thus forever incomplete. We recognize the ways in which we are still in formation and unable to see the whole of every picture. The people who have influenced us include students, professors, family, and sage individuals we met along the journey. Our formation continues with our pursuit of justice.

Lastly, we acknowledge and sincerely thank those who have gone before us and those who walk alongside us. We are truly products of the people who bless and challenge us. We are forever in pursuit of having new eyes to see and new ears to hear with a consistent acknowledgment of the ways in which we know we fall short. Our family, friends, and colleagues are essential parts of who we are and who we hope to become.

Notes

Preface

1. Frantz Fanon, *The Wretched of the Earth* (New York: Grove Press, 1963), 5.
2. la paperson, *A Third University Is Possible* (Minneapolis: University of Minnesota Press, 2017), x.
3. paperson, xvii.

Introduction

1. la paperson, *A Third University Is Possible* (Minneapolis: University of Minnesota Press, 2017), xvii.
2. Mitch Landrieu, "These statues are not just stone and metal," Twitter, June 12, 2020, https://twitter.com/mitchlandrieu/status/1271483113043099648.
3. Avery F. Gordon, *Ghostly Matters: Haunting and the Sociological Imagination* (Minneapolis: University of Minnesota Press, 2011), xvi.
4. Linda Tuhiwai Smith, *Decolonizing Methodologies: Research and Indigenous Peoples* (New York: St. Martin's Press, 1999).
5. Gordon, *Ghostly Matters*, 19.
6. Albert Memmi, *The Colonizer and the Colonized* (Boston: Beacon Press, 1991).
7. Eve Tuck and K. Wayne Yang, "Unbecoming Claims: Pedagogies of Refusal in Qualitative Research," *Qualitative Inquiry* 20, no. 6 (2014): 811–818. https://doi.org/10.1177/1077800414530265.
8. paperson, *A Third University*, 4.
9. Christopher S. Collins and Alexander Jun, *White Evolution: The Constant Struggle for Racial Consciousness* (New York: Peter Lang Publishing, 2020). In *White Evolution*, we use the term Whitefluenza to provide a metaphor for how supremacy evolves, and to construct a notion of how a kind of herd immunity can emerge from a collective critical racial consciousness. In this way an evolution toward justice rather than supremacy can offer hope for the future.
10. paperson, 10.
11. Willie James Jennings, *After Whiteness: An Education in Belonging* (Grand Rapids, MI: William B. Eerdmans Publishing Company, 2020), 9.

12 paperson, xiii.
13 Yuval Noah Harari, *Sapiens: A Brief History of Humankind* (New York: Vintage Publishing, 2015).
14 See more on the idea of the maintenance of reality and dealing with competing definitions of reality through nihilation or assimilation. Peter Berger and Thomas Luckmann, *The Social Construction of Reality*.
15 Harari, *Sapiens*.
16 Harari.
17 Harari, 304.
18 Boaventura de Sousa Santos, *Epistemologies of the South: Justice against Epistemicide* (London: Routledge, 2016).
19 Santos, 172.
20 paperson, xxii.

Chapter 1   Tools of Invasion

1 Yuval Noah Harari, *Sapiens: A Brief History of Humankind* (New York: Vintage Publishing, 2015), 237.
2 la paperson, *A Third University Is Possible* (Minneapolis: University of Minnesota Press, 2017), 5, 10.
3 Frederick Cooper and Ann Laura Stoler, eds., *Tensions of Empire: Colonial Cultures in a Bourgeois World* (Berkeley: University of California Press, 2009), 165.
4 Edward W. Said, *Culture and Imperialism* (New York: Vintage Books, 1994), 221–222.
5 Eve Tuck and K. Wayne Yang, "Unbecoming Claims: Pedagogies of Refusal in Qualitative Research," *Qualitative Inquiry* 20, no. 6 (2014): 811–818, https://doi.org/10.1177/1077800414530265.
6 Margaret D. Jacobs, "Maternal Colonialism: White Women and Indigenous Child Removal in the American West and Australia, 1880–1940," Faculty Publications, Department of History 11 (2005), "https://digitalcommons.unl.edu/historyfacpub/11" https://digitalcommons.unl.edu/historyfacpub/11; and Margaret D. Jacobs, *White Mother to a Dark Race: Settler Colonialism, Maternalism, and the Removal of Indigenous Children in the American West and Australia, 1880–1940* (Lincoln: University of Nebraska Press, 2011), 456.
7 Tiffany Lethabo King, "Interview with Dr. Tiffany Lethabo King," *Feral Feminisms* no. 4 (2015): 64, accessed September 9, 2021, https://feralfeminisms.com/lethabo-king/.
8 For the concept of the sacred canopy, see Peter L. Berger, *The Sacred Canopy: Elements of a Sociological Theory of Religion* (New York: Anchor, 1991). The quoted segment is from Harari, *Sapiens*, 210.
9 For more on metonymic reason and the accompanying dualities that limit choices and rationalities, see Boaventura de Sousa Santos, *Epistemologies of the South: Justice against Epistemicide* (London: Routledge, 2016).
10 "Sublimus Dei on the Enslavement and Evangelization of Indians," Papal Encyclicals, July 28, 2017, https://www.papalencyclicals.net/paul03/p3subli.htm.
11 Chancellor Williams, *The Destruction of Black Civilization: Great Issues of a Race from 4500 B.C. to 2000 A.D.* (Chicago: Third World Press, 1987), 56.
12 Williams, 138.

13 Mark Mathabane, *Kaffir Boy: The True Story of a Black Youth's Coming of Age in Apartheid South Africa* (New York: Macmillan, 1986), 58.
14 Cain Hope Felder, *Troubling Biblical Waters: Race, Class, and Family* (Maryknoll, NY: Orbis Books, 1998).
15 Williams, 189.
16 Cornel West, *Prophesy Deliverance!: An Afro-American Revolutionary Christianity* (Louisville, KY: Westminster John Knox Press, 2003), 28.
17 Harari, 19.
18 Williams, 56.
19 Williams, 56.
20 Santos, 91.
21 Santos, 123.
22 Cooper and Stoler, 7.
23 Harari, 278, 274.
24 Harari, 113.
25 Santos, 92.
26 Santos, 173.
27 Nancy Stepan, *The Idea of Race in Science* (Hamden, CT: Archon Books, 1982). See also Cristina Malcolmson, *Studies of Skin Color in the Early Royal Society: Boyle, Cavendish, Swift* (London: Routledge, 2016).
28 Ibram X. Kendi, *Stamped from the Beginning: The Definitive History of Racist Ideas in America* (Queens, NY: Bold Type Books, 2017), 55.
29 Stepan, 45.
30 Malcolmson, 9.
31 Santos, 190.
32 Harari, 304.
33 Harari, 274.
34 Cedric Robinson, *Black Marxism* (Chapel Hill: University of North Carolina Press, 1983), 24.
35 Eduardo Galeano, *Open Veins of Latin America: Five Centuries of the Pillage of a Continent* (New York: Monthly Review Press, 1997), 13.
36 "Requerimiento—Monarquia Espanola," Ciudad Seva, accessed September 9, 2021, https://web.archive.org/web/20070501102909/http://www.ciudadseva.com/textos/otros/requeri.htm.
37 Robinson, 67.
38 Robinson, 67.
39 Santos, 130.
40 William Easterly, *The Tyranny of Experts: Economists, Dictators, and the Forgotten Rights of the Poor* (New York: Basic Books, 2021).

Chapter 2   Homeland, Diaspora, and Traveling Whiteness

1 Craig Steven Wilder, *Ebony and Ivy: Race, Slavery, and the Troubled History of America's Universities* (London: Bloomsbury, 2013), 207, 117.
2 Chanda Prescod-Weinstein, *The Disordered Cosmos: A Journey into Dark Matter, Spacetime, & Dreams Deferred* (Queens, NY: Bold Type Books, 2021), 101.
3 Nikolaus Mani, "Jean Riolan II (1580–1657) and Medical Research," *Bulletin of the History of Medicine* 42, no. 2 (1968): 121–144.

4   Andrew S. Curran, *The Anatomy of Blackness: Science & Slavery in an Age of Enlightenment* (Baltimore, MD: Johns Hopkins University Press, 2011), 6.
5   Patrick Wolfe, *Traces of History: Elementary Structures of Race* (Brooklyn, NY: Verso, 2016), 117.
6   Charles M. Mills, *The Racial Contract* (Syracuse, NY: Cornell University Press, 1997), 32–33.
7   David Theo Goldberg, *The Racial State* (Hoboken, NJ: Wiley-Blackwell, 2002), 112.
8   Wilder, 182.
9   Juana Bordas, *Salsa, Soul, and Spirit: Leadership for a Multicultural Age,* 2nd edition (Oakland, CA: Berrett-Koehler Publishers, 2012), 20.
10 Harvey Wasserman, *America Born & Reborn* (New York: Macmillan, 1983), 277.
11 Ranginui Walker, *Ka Whawhai Tonu Matou: Struggle without End* (Auckland, NZ: Penguin, 2004), 14.
12 Edward William Bovill, *The Golden Trade of the Moors* (London: Oxford University Press, 1958), 87.
13 Bovill, 87.
14 J. W. Powell, "From Savagery to Barbarism. Annual Address of the President, J. W. Powell, Delivered February 3, 1885," *Transactions of the Anthropological Society of Washington* 3 (1885): 173–196. http://www.jstor.org/stable/658190.
15 Cedric J. Robinson, *Black Marxism: The Making of the Black Radical Tradition* (Chapel Hill: The University of North Carolina Press, 1983), 16.
16 Mills, 35.
17 Robinson, 9.
18 Linda Tuhiwai Smith, *Decolonizing Methodologies: Research and Indigenous People* (Dunedin, New Zealand: University of Otago Press, 1999), 1.
19 Marie Battiste, James Youngblood, and James Henderson, *Protecting Indigenous Knowledge and Heritage: A Global Challenge* (Saskatoon, SK: Purich Publishing Ltd., 2000).
20 Beverly Bailey, "A White Paper on Aboriginal Education," *Canadian Ethnic Studies Journal* 32, no. 1 (2000): 126–135.
21 Gregory Cajete, *Native Science: Natural Laws of Interdependence.* (Santa Fe, NM: Clear Light Publishers, 2000).
22 Sarah Maddison, *The Colonial Fantasy: Why White Australia Can't Solve Black Problems* (New South Wales: Allen & Unwin, 2019), 216.
23 Maddison, 216.
24 Raj Patel and Jason Moore, *The History of the World and Seven Cheap Things: A Guide to Capitalism, Nature, and the Future of the Planet* (Oakland, CA: UC Press, 2018).
25 Saul Dubow, *Apartheid: 1948–1994* (New York: Oxford University Press, 2014).
26 Jo-Ann Archibald, *Indigenous Storywork: Educating the Heart, Mind, Body, and Spirit* (Vancouver: University of British Columbia Press, 2008), 7.

Chapter 3   The University as Colonizer and Carrier of White Dominance

1   Paolo Freire, *Pedagogy of the Oppressed* (London: Continuum Publishing, 2007, 78).
2   Richard H. Pratt, "'Kill the Indian, and Save the Man': Capt. Richard H. Pratt on the Education of Native Americans." History Matters - The U.S. Survey Course on the Web. Accessed October 29, 2022. http://historymatters.gmu.edu/d/4929/.
3   Boaventura de Sousa Santos, *The End of the Cognitive Empire: The Coming of Age of Epistemologies of the South* (Durham, NC: Duke University Press, 2018).

4   Santos, 6.
5   Charles King, *Gods of the Upper Air: How a Circle of Renegade Anthropologists Reinvented Race, Sex, and Gender in the Twentieth Century* (New York: Doubleday, 2019), 27–28.
6   J. W. Powell, "From Savagery to Barbarism. Annual Address of the President, J. W. Powell, Delivered February 3, 1885." Transactions of the Anthropological Society of Washington 3, 173–196, http://www.jstor.org/stable/658190.
7   Harold Perkin, "History of Universities," eds. James J. F. Forest and Philip G. Altbach, *International Handbook of Higher Education* (New York: Springer, 2007), 159.
8   Simon Marginson, "Introduction," *The Globalization of Higher Education*, eds. Roger King, Simon Marginson, and Rajani Naidoo (Cheltenham, UK: Edward Elgar Publishing, 2013), 3.
9   Phillip G. Altbach, *Global Perspectives, Higher Education* (Baltimore, MD: Johns Hopkins University Press, 2016), 201.
10 Marginson, 4.
11 Piya Chatterjee and Sunaina Maira, "Introduction. The Imperial University: Rae War and the Nation State," *The Imperial University: Academic Repression and Scholarly Dissent* (Minneapolis: University of Minnesota Press, 2014), 14.
12 Chatterjee and Maira, 14.
13 Boaventura de Sousa Santos, *Epistemologies of the South: Justice Against Epistemicide* (London: Routledge, 2014), 10.
14 Santos, *Epistemologies of the South*, 10.
15 Boaventura de Sousa Santos, "Human Rights as an Emancipatory Script? Cultural and Political Conditions," in *Another Knowledge Is Possible: Beyond Northern Epistemologies* (Brooklyn, NY: Verso Books, 2007), 6–7.
16 Deborah A. Thomas and Kamari Maxine Clarke, "Introduction. Globalization and the Transformations," in *Globalization and Race: Transformations in the Cultural Production of Blackness*, eds. Kamari Maxine Clarke and Deborah A. Thomas (Durham, NC: Duke University Press, 2006), 2.
17 Jack Goody, *The Theft of History* (Cambridge: Cambridge University Press, 2006), 1.
18 Ibram X. Kendi, *Stamped from the Beginning: The Definitive History of Racist Ideas in America* (New York: Nation Books, 2016), 17.
19 Herodotus 425 BCE *The Histories* Book II, sections 50–51, trans. A. D. Godley (Cambridge, MA: Harvard University Press, 1920).
20 Prince A. Cuba, "Foreword," *Stolen Legacy: The Egyptian Origins of Western Philosophy*, reprint of a book review for *Your Black Books Guide* 1, no. 9 (July 1990).
21 George M. James, *Stolen Legacy: The Egyptian Origins of Western Philosophy* (Brattleboro, VT: Allegro Books, 2017), 27.
22 James, 42.
23 James, 199.
24 Chancellor Williams, *The Destruction of Black Civilization: Great Issues of a Race from 4500 B.C. to 2000 A.D.* (Chicago: Third World Press, 1987), 189.
25 Bryan W. Van Norden, *Taking Back Philosophy: A Multicultural Manifesto* (New York: Columbia University Press, 2017), 21.
26 James, 199.
27 Shive Visvanathan, *A Carnival for Science: Essays on Science, Technology and Development* (Delhi: Oxford University Press, 1997), 20.

28 Craig Steven Wilder, *Ebony and Ivy: Race, Slavery, and the Troubled History of America's Universities* (London: Bloomsbury, 2013), 183.
29 Cristina Malcolmson, *Studies of Skin Color and the Early Royal Society: Boyle, Cavendish, Swift* (London: Routledge, 2016), 4.
30 Malcomson, 31.
31 Kendi, 55
32 Wilder.
33 Kendi, 109.
34 Wilder, 182.
35 Nancy Leys Stepan, *The Idea of Race* (Hamden, CT: Archon Books, 1982).
36 Wilder, 199.
37 Wilder, 199.
38 Wilder, 225.
39 Wilder, 228.
40 Stepan, *The Idea of Race*, 41.
41 Tukufu Zuberi, *Thicker than Blood: How Racial Statistics Lie* (Minneapolis: University of Minnesota Press, 2003), 33.
42 Zuberi, 35.
43 Quoted in Nancy Leys Stepan, *The Hour of Eugenics: Race, Gender, and Nation in Latin America* (Syracuse, NY: Cornell University Press, 1991), 28.
44 Stepan, *The Hour of Eugenics*, 171.
45 Tukufu Zuberi and Eduardo Bonilla-Silva, eds., *White Logic, White Methods: Racism and Methodology* (Lanham, MD: Rowman & Littlefield, 2008), 7.
46 Zuberi and Bonilla-Silva, 17–18.
47 Gloria Ladson-Billings, *Racialized Discourses and Ethnic Epistemologies*, eds. Norman K. Denzin and Yvonna S. Lincoln, *Handbook of Qualitative Research*, 2nd ed. (Thousand Oaks, CA: SAGE, 2000), 271.

Chapter 4   Dominant White Minorities and Invasion in Southern Africa

1 Olajumoke Yacob-Haliso, Ngozi Nwogwugwu, and Gift Ntiwunka, *African Indigenous Knowledges in a Postcolonial World* (London: Routledge, 2021), 11.
2 Christi van der Westhuizen, *White Power & The Rise and Fall of the National Party* (Cape Town: Zebra Press, 2007), 11.
3 Saul Dubow, *Apartheid: 1948–1994* (New York: Oxford University Press, 2014), 7, 8, 10.
4 Dubow, 3.
5 Jacques Pauw, *Into the Heart of the Whore: The Story of Apartheid's Death Squads* (Gauteng, SA: Jonathan Ball, 2017), 251–252.
6 Westhuizen, Christi van der, 16.
7 Much of this section on the history of the business practices of Wernher, Beit, and Rhodes leaned upon the work of Raymond E. Dumett and his edited volume titled *Mining Tycoons in the Age of Empire, 1870–1945: Entrepreneurship, High Finance, Politics, and Territorial Expansion* (London: Routledge, 2009), 85–95.
8 Westhuizen, Christi van der, 12.
9 Cecil J. Rhodes, *Confession of Faith*, (1877) https://pages.uoregon.edu/kimball/Rhodes-Confession.htm. Accessed June 1, 2021.
10 Yacob-Haliso, Nwogwugwu, and Ntiwunka, 2.

11. Toyin Falola and Christian Jennings, *Africanizing Knowledge: African Studies Across the Disciplines* (New Brunswick, NJ: Transaction Publishers, 2002).
12. Mahmood Mamdani, *Neither Settler Nor Native: The Making and Unmaking of Permanent Minorities* (Cambridge: Belknap Press of Harvard University Press, 2020), 144.

Chapter 5   Shades of Advantage in Brazil

1. Eduardo Galeano, *Open Veins of Latin America: Five Centuries of the Pillage of a Continent* (New York: Monthly Review Press, 1997), 1.
2. Eli Leão Catachunga, Rosana Maria Pires Barbato Schwartz, and Renan Antônio da Silva, "O povo Ticuna sob uma perspectiva histórica: de suas origens mitológicas à perda de sua identidade," *Revista Sem Aspas* 10, no. 00 (2021): e021006, https://doi.org/10.29373/sas.v10i00.15163, 6–7.
3. Boris Fausto and Sergio Fausto, *A Concise History of Brazil* 2nd ed. (Cambridge: Cambridge University Press, 2014), 10.
4. S. Buarque de Holanda, *Roots of Brazil* (Notre Dame, IN: University of Notre Dame Press, [1936] 2012, 24.
5. Fausto and Fausto, 18.
6. De Holanda, 36.
7. De Holanda, 58–59.
8. Fausto and Fausto, 28.
9. Fausto and Fausto, 49.
10. Fausto and Fausto, 47.
11. Edward E. Telles, *Pigmentocracies: Ethnicity, Race, and Color in Latin America* (Chapel Hill: The University of North Carolina Press, 2014), 21; France Winddance Twine, *Racism in a Racial Democracy: The Maintenance of White Supremacy in Brazil* (New Brunswick, NJ, Rutgers University Press, 1998), 59; Barbara Weinstein, *The Color of Modernity: São Paulo and the Making of Race and Nation in Brazil* (Durham, NC: Duke University Press, 2015).
12. Edward E. Telles, *Race in Another America: The Significance of Skin Color in Brazil* (Princeton, NJ: Princeton University Press, 2006), 10.
13. Ollie Johnson III and Rosana Heringer, *Race, Politics and Education in Brazil: Affirmative Action in Higher Education* (New York: Palgrave Macmillan, 2015), 1.
14. Johnson III and Heringer, 1.
15. Nancy Leys Stepan, *The Hour of Eugenics: Race, Gender, and Nation in Latin America* (Syracuse, NY: Cornell University Press, 1991), 45–47.
16. Stepan, 42.
17. Stepan, 48–49.
18. "100 Years of the Decease of Arnaldo Vieira De Carvalho, Founder and First Director of the Medical School of USP," University of São Paulo, January 6, 2020, https://www.fm.usp.br/en/news/100-years-of-the-decease-of-arnaldo-vieira-de-carvalho-founder-and-first-director-of-the-medical-school-of-usp.
19. Luisa Farah Schwartzman and Angela Randolpho Paiva, "Not Just Racial Quotas: Affirmative Action in Brazilian Higher Education 10 Years Later," *British Journal of Sociology* 37, no. 4 (2014): 4.
20. Rosana Heringer, "Expectations about Higher Education in City of God, Brazil: Does Diversification in Access Make a Difference?" International Sociology

Association 2nd Forum of Sociology: *Social Justice & Democratization* (Buenos Aires, 2012), 4.
21. Leone Campos de Sousa and Paulo Nascimento, "Brazilian National Identity at a Crossroads: The Myth of Racial Democracy at the Development of Black Identity," *International Journal of Politics, Culture, and Society* 19, no. 3/4 (2008): 129–143; Rosana Heringer, "Outcomes and Challenges of Affirmative Action Policies and Expansion of Higher Education in Brazil (2007–2012)," Congress of the Latin American Studies Association in Washington, D.C., 2013.
22. Sarah Lempp, "With the Eyes of Society? Doing Race in Affirmative Action Practices in Brazil," *Citizenship Studies* 23, no. 7 (2019): 703–719.
23. G. Reginald Daniel, *Race and Multiraciality in Brazil and the United States: Converging Paths?* (University Park, PA: Penn State University Press, 2006), 53.
24. Carolina Maria de Jesus, *Child of the Dark: The Diary of Carolina Maria de Jesus* (New York, Signet Classics, [1962] 2003), 30.
25. Jaime Amparo Alves, *The Anti-Black City: Police Terror and Black Urban Life in Brazil* (Minneapolis: University of Minnesota Press, 2018), 170.
26. Twine, 59.
27. Gilberto Freyre, *The Masters and the Slaves: A Study in the Development of Brazilian Civilization* (Berkeley: University of California Press, 1986).
28. Johnson III and Heringer, 2.
29. "National Curriculum Parameters Secondary Education," Brazil Ministry of Education, accessed October 21, 2021, http://portal.mec.gov.br/seb/arquivos/pdf/pcning.pdf.
30. Melissa Nobles, *Shades of Citizenship: Race and the Census in Modern Politics* (Stanford, CA, Stanford University Press, 2000), 156.
31. Nobles, 156.
32. Nobles, 157.
33. Nobles, 158.
34. Frantz Fanon, *The Wretched of the Earth* (New York: Grove Press, [1963] 2004), 34.
35. International Work Group for Indigenous Affairs, accessed October 21, 2021, https://www.iwgia.org/en/brazil.html.

Chapter 6   Empty Treaties and Occupied Land in Oceania

1. Epeli Hau'ofa, *We Are the Ocean: Selected Works* (Honolulu: University of Hawaii Press, 2008), 29.
2. Nicholas Thomas, *Voyagers: The Settlement of the Pacific* (London: Head of Zeus, 2021), 79–80.
3. Ranginui Walker, *Ka Whawhai Tonu Matou: Struggle without End* (Auckland, NZ: Penguin, 2004), 14.
4. Serge Tcherzerkoff, "A Long and Unfortunate Voyage towards the 'Invention' of the Melanesia/Polynesia Distinction 1595–1832," trans. Isabel Ollivier. *The Journal of Pacific History* 38, no. 2 (2003): 175–196, https://doi.org/10.1080/0022334032000120521.
5. Richard Broome, *Aboriginal Australians* (Sydney: Allen & Lunwin, 2019), 283.
6. Broome, 16.
7. Warwick P. Anderson, *The Cultivation of Whiteness: Science, Health, and Racial Destiny in Australia* (Durham, NC: Duke University Press, 2006), 4.

8 Anderson, 2.
9 Anderson, 4.
10 T. P. MacDonald, "Tropical Lands and White Races," *Transactions of the Royal Society of Tropical Medicine and Hygiene* 1 (1907): 201–214, https://doi.org/10.1016/s0035-9203(07)90029-2.
11 MacDonald, 214.
12 Anderson, 253.
13 Anderson, 255.
14 Margaret D. Jacobson, Margaret D. *White Mother to a Dark Race: Settler Colonialism, Maternalism, and the Removal of Indigenous Children in the American West and Australia, 1880–1940* (Lincoln, NE: University of Nebraska Press, 2009).
15 H. E. Barff, *Short Historical Account of the University of Sydney* (Syndey: Angus and Robertson, 1902), 5–6.
16 Barff, 6.
17 William Charles Wentworth, *A Statistical, Historical, and Political Description of the Colony of New South Wales, and Its Dependent Settlements in Van Diemen's Land, Etc.* (London: G. & W. B. Whittaker, 1819), 4–5.
18 Renee Gorman, "Wentworth Must Stand," Institute of Public Affairs, June 28, 2019, https://ipa.org.au/publications-ipa/wentworth-must-stand.
19 Lyn Turnbull, "Wingara-Mura Design Principles," *South Sydney Herald*, June 21, 2019, https://southsydneyherald.com.au/wingara-mura-design-principles/.
20 The Ramsay Centre, "About the Ramsay Centre," accessed May 20, 2020, https://www.ramsaycentre.org/about-us/.
21 "I'm Still Not a Racist, But . . . ," National Tertiary Education Union, October 4, 2018, http://www.nteu.org.au/article/Report-release—I%27m-still-not-a-racist%2C-but . . . -20943.
22 John White, *Ancient History of the Maori, His Mythology and Traditions* (Government Printing, Wellington, 1888), 128–129.
23 Augustus Earle, *A Narrative of a Nine Months' Residence in New Zealand* (London: Longman, Rees, Orme, Brown, Green & Longman, 1832), 253–254.
24 Vincent O'Malley, Wally Penetito, and Bruce Stirling, *The Treaty of Waitangi Companion: Maori and Pakeha from Tasman to Today* (Auckland, NZ: Auckland University Press, 2014), 25.
25 O'Malley, Penetito, and Sterling, 56.
26 Walker, 147.
27 Don Rowe, "Open Letter Claims White Supremacy and 'Climate of Fear' at University of Auckland," The Spinoff website, April 11, 2019, https://thespinoff.co.nz/society/12-04-2019/open-letter-claims-white-supremacy-and-climate-of-fear-at-university-of-auckland/.
28 Rowe.
29 Rowe.
30 Katie Scotcher, "Open Letter Denounces White Supremacy at Auckland University," October 2, 2019, https://www.rnz.co.nz/news/national/400168/open-letter-denounces-white-supremacy-at-auckland-university.
31 la paperson, *A Third University Is Possible* (Minneapolis: University of Minnesota Press, 2017), 44.
32 Story of Awanuiārangi. Accessed October 30, 2023, https://www.wananga.ac.nz/about/story-of-awanuiarangi/chapter-eight/.

Conclusion

1. la paperson, *A Third University Is Possible* (Minneapolis: University of Minnesota Press, 2017), xvii, xxiii.
2. Lao Tzu, *Tao Te Ching* (New York: Vintage Books, 1972), 1.
3. Roland Barthes, *Mythologies* (Paris: Editions du Seuil, 1957), 262.
4. Toni Morrison, *The Origin of Others* (Cambridge, MA: Harvard University Press, 2017), 6.
5. Audre Lorde, *The Collected Poems of Audre Lorde* (New York: W. W. Norton, 2000), 59.
6. paperson, 6.
7. paperson, 6.
8. Ghassan Hage, "White Entitlement Is Part of the Very Structure of Australian Society," *The Guardian*, March 17, 2019, https://www.theguardian.com/commentisfree/2019/mar/18/white-entitlement-is-part-of-the-very-structure-of-australian-society.
9. Paul Karp, "Australia Considers Fast-Track Visas for White South African Farmers," *The Guardian*, March 14, 2018, https://www.theguardian.com/australia-news/2018/mar/14/dutton-considers-fast-track-visas-for-white-south-african-farmers.
10. Paul Karp, "South Africa Hails 'Retraction' of Australian Minister's Offer to White Farmers," *The Guardian*, April 3, 2018, https://www.theguardian.com/world/2018/apr/03/south-africa-hails-retraction-of-australian-ministers-offer-to-white-farmers.
11. paperson, xv.
12. This article has a very thorough literature review, synthesis, and dissection of definitions and strategies toward decolonizing the curriculum. It includes key literature covering the regions addressed in this book and the particularities of decolonizing work in relation to indigeneity. See Riyad A. Shahjahan, et al., "'Decolonizing' Curriculum and Pedagogy: A Comparative Review Across Disciplines and Global Higher Education Contexts," *Review of Educational Research* (September 2021), https://doi.org/10.3102/00346543211042423.
13. Harry H. Laughlin, *The Second International Exhibition of Eugenics*, American Museum of Natural History, New York (Baltimore: Williams and Wilkins Company, 1923), 15, fig. 3.
14. Tukufu Zuberi and Eduardo Bonilla-Silva, *White Logic, White Methods: Racism and Methodology* (Lanham, MD: Rowman & Littlefield, 2008), 5–6.
15. paperson, 52–53.
16. Willie James Jennings, *After Whiteness: An Education in Belonging* (Grand Rapids, MI: William B. Eerdmans Publishing Company, 2020), 9.

Index

Africanization, 14, 71, 81, 86, 88
Afrikaans, 14, 37, 74, 77–78, 81–85
Afrikaners, 14, 45, 48, 51, 75–77, 87, 90
Afro Brazilian, xv, 93, 96, 103–106
Altbach, Phillip, 59
Alves, Jaime Amparo, 101
American Philosophical Society, 64
anima nullius, 25
Aotearoa, xii, 15, 44, 69, 108, 110, 114, 118, 123
apartheid, 14, 28, 51–52, 75–76, 81–82, 84, 127–128
Aristotle, 61–62
assimilation, xix, 6, 8, 23, 49, 54
Auckland University of Technology, 119

bandeirantes, 95
Bantu Education Act, 76–78
Battiste, Marie, 49
Biko, Steve, 90
Black: Africans, 10, 43, 84, 106; Brazilians, 103–104, 106; civilization(s), 25, 27, 45; ingenuity, xiii, 74, 132; islands, 109; South Africans, xii, 48, 51, 76–77, 81, 83–87, 89, 103, 128
Boas, Franz, 56
boers, 14, 74, 76
Botany Bay, 4, 15, 47, 70, 110
Boyle, Robert, 31

Cajete, Gregory, 49
Candomblé, 93–94

Cape Town, South Africa, xii, 2, 4, 46, 70, 74, 78, 86, 126
Carvalho, Arnaldo Vieira de, 97–98, 106
Child of the Dark, 100
Civil War, 2
codified knowledge, 32, 57, 65
cognitive justice, 11, 14, 55, 67–68, 132
colorism/colorist, 4, 6, 75, 82, 84, 86, 106, 126
Columbus, Christopher, 33, 40, 44, 108
Conrad, Joseph, 84
conscientization, 117, 133
conversion, 15, 25, 92–93
Cook, James, 8, 9, 25, 109, 118, 123
Cradle of Humankind, 73–74
Curran, Andrew, 41
curriculum, 54, 67, 81, 83, 88–89, 103–104, 114, 117, 120, 127
Curse of Ham, 26, 82

Dark Ages, 34
Darwin, Charles, 9, 65
decolonize (ing, ization), 11, 73, 86–90, 105, 117, 127–128, 131
dichotomy, 12, 28
double-hulled canoe, 44, 107–108
dualistic constructions, 24
Dutch Reformed Church, 20, 46, 51, 75, 81, 83

ecosystem, xiii, 30, 32, 44, 57, 107, 129
Egypt, 9, 25
Egyptian Mystery System, 61

empiricism, 31, 63
Enlightenment, 1, 8, 14, 24, 29, 64, 67, 126, 129
Eora, 110–111
epistemicide, 4, 30, 54, 62, 68, 84, 88
Ethiopia, x, 25, 26, 45
ethnostate, 38
eugenics, 39, 48, 66–67, 96–98, 100, 106, 111, 129–130
Eurocentric, 22, 37, 57, 121

favela, 99–101
Federal University of Bahia, 93, 97
Federal University of Rio de Janeiro, 15, 96
Fees Must Fall, 135
feudalism, 34–35, 39–40, 61
financial fascism, 34
First Fleet, 4, 15, 69, 110
First Peoples, x, 9, 56, 113
Franklin, Benjamin, 64
Freyre, Gilberto, 102

Galeano, Eduardo, 35, 91
Galton, Francis, 65–66
genocide, 9, 20, 27, 30, 40, 45, 114
ghosts, 5, 7, 12, 126
globalization, 28, 33, 51, 60
Global North, 12, 55, 59–60, 130
Global South, ix, 4, 12, 24, 53, 55, 59–60, 110, 128
Gordon, Avery, 5
Group Areas Act, 76, 82
Guarani, 14

Harari, Yuval, 9–10, 27, 29
Hau'ofa, Epeli, 107
Henderson, James Youngblood, 49

imperial, 1, 3, 10, 20, 32, 52, 55, 75, 87–88
Indian boarding schools, 54
Indigenous: diaspora, 13, 52; knowledge(s) systems, 23, 32, 44, 56, 71, 73, 83–84; land, 105; peoples, 6, 15, 38–39, 47–50, 62, 83–84, 95–97, 114, 132–133
Islam, 24–25, 34, 45, 57

Jefferson, Thomas, 43, 64
Jennings, Willie, 6, 132
Johannesburg, 50, 73

Kant, Immanuel, 62
Kendi, Ibram X., 61
Khoisan, 73–74
King, Tiffany Lethobo, 23
Kipling, Rudyard, 9
knowledge production, 5, 8, 12–14, 23, 30, 43–44, 55–56, 59–61, 66–69, 110

Ladson-Billings, Gloria, 67
Lapita, 108
Lorde, Audre, 127

Maddison, Sara, 50
Malan, D.F., 75
Mamdani, Mahmood, 89
mana, 69, 107–108
Mandela, Nelson, 78, 82, 103–104
Mansa Musa, 45
Marginson, Simon, 58–59
Maria de Jesus, Carolina, 100
Mathabane, Mark, 25
Melanesia, 109–110
metonymic, 29, 31
Mills, Charles R., 41
missionary, 24–26, 51, 111, 118, 123
Mixed Marriages Act, 29, 76
monoculture, 30, 60
monogenesis, 26, 30–31, 65
monotheism, 2–9, 24–26, 46
Morrison, Toni, 126
mutation, 6–7, 26, 38

Napoleon, 9, 29
National Party (South Africa), 75
Native homelands, 52
Native Schools Act, 119
Nubia, 26

objective knowledge, 6, 23, 62

Pākehā, xii, 118–120
Pearson, Karl, 65
Peterson, Hector, 84–85
phrenology, 31, 39
polygenesis, 26, 30–31, 39
Polynesia, 109–110
polytheism, 7–8, 24
poverty, x, xi, 34
Powell, J. W., 56

Pratt, Richard H., 54
Prescod-Weinstein, Chanda, 40
proselytizing, 7, 9, 132
pseudoscience, 29, 40–41, 48, 82, 96–97, 99, 111, 113, 117, 129
Pythagoras, 61

quilombo, 106

racial capitalism, 35, 39
racial classification, 30, 48, 50, 96, 98–99
Racial Contract, 41
racial determinism, 65
racial state, 43
racial statistics, 66
Reformation, 40, 62
rematriation, 71, 128
Renaissance, 8
Requerimiento, 33
Rhodes, Cecil John, 2, 50, 75, 79, 85, 106
Rhodes Must Fall, 2, 85, 126
Rio de Janeiro, Brazil, xvi, 4, 15, 94–96, 99–100, 104–106
Robinson, Cedric, 34
Rodrigues, Raimundo Nina, 97
Royal Society, 8, 31–32, 63–66

sacred canopy, 24
salvation, 24
Santos, Boaventura de Sousa, 59–60
São Paulo, Brazil, 95, 99–100, 105–106
São Paulo Eugenics Society, 97–98, 106
scientific revolution, 4, 8, 13, 29, 32, 62, 64
settler colonialism, ix, x, 5–8, 12–14, 19–20, 34, 50, 78, 85, 88–89, 126, 133
Smith, Linda Tuhiwai, 5, 48, 69
Sobukwe, Robert, 90
social justice, 11, 60, 67, 132

Soweto, 84–85
statues, 86, 117, 127
Stellenbosch University, 14, 78, 81–83
sterilization, 66, 97
syncretism, 9–10, 93, 118

Tao Te Ching, 125
terra nullius, 25, 110–111, 118
Te Whare Wānanga o Awanuiārangi, 119, 123
Tikuna, 91–92
Treaty of Waitangi, 110, 118–121

Universidade Federal do Rio de Janeiro, 15, 96
University of Auckland, 119–122
University of Cape Town (UCT), 2, 78–79, 85, 106, 126
University of São Paulo, 97–98
University of Sydney, xix, 113–117
University of the Western Cape, 78

verification commissions, 99
Verwoerd, H.F., 76–77, 82

Wentworth, William, xx, 50, 113
Wentworth Must Fall, 116
Western science, 31, 55, 60
White: Afrikaners, 51, 75, 77, 83; Australia, 112, 117, 127; entitlement, 127; homeland, 4, 35, 38, 40, 43, 46, 50–53, 126; identity, 13, 47, 74; logic, 46–47, 67, 89, 116; methods, 67; normativity, 15, 31, 130; power, 26, 132; settlers, 50, 78–79, 118; South African, xix, 85–87, 90, 127
Wilder, Craig Steven, 43
Williams, Chancellor, 25, 27
Wolfe, Patrick, 41

About the Authors

CHRISTOPHER S. COLLINS studies the function of organizations in society and the production of knowledge in diverse and global settings. In collaboration with people around the world he has worked on studies of the World Bank and poverty reduction, the social value of higher education in the Asia Pacific region, and Indigenous knowledges in Hawai'i. For many years he worked with doctoral students to think deeply about cognitive justice and the interdependence and ecology of knowledges. He has completed more than fifty scholarly products (books, journal articles, and chapters), including his latest book, *White Evolution: The Constant Struggle for Racial Consciousness*, coauthored with Alexander Jun. He earned a PhD from the University of California, Los Angeles, but learned much more from teachers, mentors, friends, and guides who did not offer course credit or diplomas. Currently he is teaching organizational behavior at Pepperdine University.

CHRISTOPHER B. NEWMAN focuses his research primarily on outcomes, inequities, and undergraduate student experiences in science, technology, engineering, and mathematics (STEM). Additionally, he has interests in multicultural education in global contexts. Newman has served as a consultant to the National Science Foundation's Colloquy on Minority Males. He has coauthored or coedited four books including *Comprehensive Multicultural Education in the 21st Century*. His research has appeared in the *Journal of Multicultural Education*, Teachers College Record, the *Journal of Social Issues*, *Journal of Women and Minorities in Science and Engineering*, *Journal of Research in Science Teaching*, *The Journal of Negro Education*, and *Urban Education* among others. He earned several awards while a faculty member at the University of San Diego, including an Outstanding Teaching Award (2013) and the Faculty Trailblazer award for mentorship and support of Black college students (2018).

ALEXANDER JUN conducts research on equity and justice in higher education around the world. A TEDx speaker in 2012, Jun was also a global fellow with the Center for Khmer Studies in Cambodia in 2010; an international research fellow at Curtin University in Perth, Australia, in 2016; and a 2018 scholar in residence at Belmont University in Tennessee. Jun is associate editor of the *Journal of Behavioral and Social Sciences*, and author of *From Here to University: Access, Mobility, and Resilience among Urban Latino Youth*. He also coauthored *White Out: Understanding White Privilege and Dominance in the Modern Age*, *White Jesus: The Architecture of Racism in Religion and Education*, and *White Evolution: The Constant Struggle for Racial Consciousness* (2020).